Rewrite Right!

Rewrite Right!

How to Revise Your Way to Better Writing

Jan Venolia

Author of <u>Write Right!</u> and <u>Better Letters</u>

Ten Speed Press/Periwinkle Press

1🅡
TEN SPEED PRESS
P. O. Box 7123
Berkeley, California 94707

Illustrations by Carol Venolia
Cover Design by Hal Hershey
Typesetting by *turnaround*, Berkeley

Library of Congress Cataloging-in-Publication Data

Venolia, Jan.
    Rewrite right!

    Bibliography: p. 191
    1. English language—Business English.   2. English
language—Rhetoric.   3. English language—Style.
4. Editing.I. Title.
PE1479.B87V46 1987   808'.066651   86-30177
ISBN 0-89815-202-X

Printed in the United States of America

1 2 3 4 5 — 91 90 89 88 87

Mend your speech a little, lest it mar your fortune.
—Shakespeare

... Mend your writing, too.
—Jan Venolia

Contents

Chapter 1

Let's Get Acquainted

Chapter 1.
LET'S GET ACQUAINTED

Rewrite Right! is for people in business and government who must write as part of their jobs and for freelance writers struggling to make sales. It's a handbook on editing and revising, but it's also about writing.

Editing is improving something written—making it easier to follow, snappier, more interesting. Knowing how to edit means knowing what makes writing good in the first place. And good writing comes from knowing how to revise, how to pull and adjust words until they say what they're intended to say. In other words, writing and editing are two facets of the same subject: doing a good job of putting ideas into words.

Is Good Writing Obsolete?

Who cares about good writing these days? Has the need for good writing disappeared as paper and pencil are replaced by screen and printout? Not at all. In fact, when asked recently what subjects students should study to prepare them for business, top executives answered in one voice: Learn to write better. Editors who must sift through mailbags full of ineptly written manuscripts would say, "Amen."

Many skilled individuals falter when it comes to writing. They may be experts at high-energy physics or marketing, but tell them to write it up and they turn into wimps. They mask their insecurity by relying on the worn-out expressions and stilted prose they perceive as being authoritative. For writing models they look to their colleagues, most of whom write poorly.

Such mediocre writing can have unwelcome effects. Muddled instructions create confusion. Costly research is repeated because the results were buried in an obscure, two-pound report. Boring writing is tossed aside unread, a waste of the investment made in producing it. Slipshod writing breeds distrust, prompting readers to wonder if language is the writer's only area of incompetence.

At the other end of the spectrum, good writing can get things done right. Its crisp, clear style requires less of the reader's time. Good writing is *cost-effective*; it lowers administrative expenses and lightens workloads. Polished writing has a professional tone that reflects well on the general competence of the writer, suggesting that attention is paid to other areas as well.

Will Another Book Help?

The reference shelves of bookstores and libraries are crowded with books offering to help people write better. Do we need another? To me, the test of a good book is first whether it covers what interests me, and second how quickly I can find that information. Many handbooks fail on both counts. They devote space to subjects that are only obliquely interesting to the modern writer and editor while omitting others that would be useful. And an astonishing number of books contain a rudimentary index or none at all. Using them requires either that you memorize the contents or that you waste time flipping through the pages trying to find what you're looking for.

As a writing consultant, I have learned what kind of help most people need. They want a reference that doesn't burden them with useless information; they want answers to their questions in simple, direct language. My previous books, *Write Right!* and *Better Letters*, provide such help. *Rewrite Right!* is for those who want a more thorough treatment of the ways to improve writing. It goes into the subjects covered in *Write Right!* in greater depth; it broadens the principles of style presented in *Better Letters*. It includes a chapter on removing bias from writing, a subject of concern to many writers and editors. Furthermore, *Rewrite Right!* is a product of the computer age. It acknowledges, in content and approach, how technology affects writing and revising today.

Some Suggestions for Using This Book

Rewrite Right! is not only for those who write and revise their own work but also for those who are asked to edit another person's writing. Although I have generally assumed that the reader is both author and editor, the information I present will also be useful to those who are editors only. In the beginning of Chapter 2, I include some thoughts about the special requirements of editing someone else's writing.

Rewrite Right! is a *refer*ence. You can refer to it to clarify a particular usage or answer specific questions as they come up. You might look up whether *its* should have an apostrophe, how to make subjects and verbs agree, or how to organize material. Or you can use it as a short course by systematically proceeding from front to back, honing your skills: ferreting out bias, catching breaks in continuity, adding starch to your words, and eliminating jargon. If you are a novice, you might want to focus first on a few basics: tailoring the writing to your audience (p. 34), removing unnecessary words (p. 66), and writing in the active voice (p. 79).

I've included a variety of reference material: lists of accepted abbreviations, hackneyed expressions, common redundancies, and irregular plurals (criteria, media). I've also suggested ways to improve the appearance of a document and explored how word processors give the writer/editor a whole new bag of tricks. If any terms I've used are unfamiliar, you'll find their definitions in the Glossary at the back of the book.

Some writing handbooks skip subjects like punctuation and usage, assuming that the readers already know how to write an adequate sentence. I make no such assumption. I know that many who are reading this book are uncertain about what makes writing good or bad. In this multiple-choice age, you may have completed your education having had little actual experience in writing. Grammar and punctuation are reminders of tedious hours spent in an uninspiring class; it might not occur to you that they could be useful tools.

Just how useful are grammar and punctuation? Do they have anything to do with modern communication? Indeed they do. If writing is to get results or to convey information, readers should be able to understand it promptly; they shouldn't have to struggle to make sense of the words. And making writing easy to understand can be as simple as putting a comma in the right place.

Today's writers needn't be intimidated by commas or confused by subject-verb agreement. Writing style used to be a way to flaunt your education—the more ornate and involved, the better. By contrast, modern usage is accessible and geared toward making writing clear and easy to understand. A refreshing logic characterizes the few rules that are needed for clear writing; the arbitrary, obfuscatory ones have fallen from grace.

The satisfactions that come from turning a chaotic jumble of words into lucid prose have few parallels. As you use *Rewrite Right!* to develop your skills, take time to enjoy the quotations that illustrate many of the rules. The words of Will Rogers and Lewis Carroll add an element of fun that will lighten what may now appear to be a chore. Along the way, you might even find that writing and rewriting become enjoyable.

> *As your experience grows you will find that revising is pleasurable, even though its purpose is the discovery of your own failings.* —Jacques Barzun

Chapter 2

Some Useful
Tools

Chapter 2.
SOME USEFUL TOOLS

Editing is like sculpting in many ways. The editor and the sculptor both take a basic form, add elements that are needed to strengthen lines or create interest, and remove elements that distract from a harmonious whole. Each step builds on what has been done before. Special tools and knowledge equip the editor and sculptor to experiment with different arrangements. This chapter presents some tools to be used in shaping and reshaping your writing.

> *Don't be afraid to seize whatever you have written and cut it to ribbons. It can always be restored to its original condition in the morning.*—E. B. White

Editing Another's Work

Editing someone else's writing is both easier and harder than editing your own. It's easier to catch places where the reader might stumble; it's harder to deal with prickly egos. Making all the changes you think necessary while remaining on friendly terms with the author requires tact. Remember that the author has already invested a lot of time, and your suggestions will probably call for an additional investment. Avoid being picky; emphasize ways to help the writer convey ideas more forcefully.

> *No passion in the world is equal to the passion to alter someone else's draft.*—H.G. Wells

First, determine the kind and amount of editing desired. Even if you are expected to use only a light touch, limited to corrections such as spelling and punctuation, you should still unmix mixed metaphors, suggest substitutes for pet words, and reposition misplaced modifiers. Your primary task is to enforce consistency—consistency in numbers, captions, format, acronyms, capitalization, compound words, and similar details that contribute to smooth, orderly writing.

Are you expected to make more drastic revisions: shifting paragraphs, rewriting the opening, clarifying fuzzy areas? If so, assume that something you find confusing or jarring will probably confuse or jar another reader, too. Ask the author to shed light on the intended meaning. You should also rein in overwritten prose, and reinforce areas where too much has been left out. Inject passion where the writing is lifeless, and cool the rhetoric where the author is carried away with cleverness. But don't insinuate your personality into the writing, making it a crazy quilt of different styles. Above all, don't change an author's meaning.

As the editor of someone else's writing, you can sniff out trouble before it gets into print. You also serve as a sounding board, the first sign of whether the author will succeed in getting the desired response. It's an important role. Handled skillfully, the author-editor synergy produces writing that neither individual could create alone.

Editing Your Own Work

Editing your own writing, on the other hand, challenges your ability to be objective. To develop distance from your writing, take a break before beginning to revise. Several days may be needed before you can evaluate your writing impartially. If you can't let it "cool off" that long, try overnight. As a minimum, walk away from it for a few moments or do something distracting—whatever is necessary to change your perceptions from those of writer to those of reader. Try to see the document with fresh eyes, as if for the first time.

> *Good writing is good manners. You can both please and help your public only when you learn how to be the first victim of your writing, how to anticipate a reader's difficulties and to hear yourself as others hear you.*—Ritchie R. Ward

As you review what you have written, you may have an uneasy sense that it needs work, but not know where to dig in. Colleagues or friends often tell you that something is wrong with certain passages but are unable to put their finger on *why* or how to remedy it. An editing checklist is a good way to start your investigation. Is the writing too stiff? Is the reader yanked around? Are transitions too abrupt? A checklist for use with this book begins on page 12.

SEPTEMBER
1
2
3
4
5
6
7
8
9
10
11
12
write report
13
14
15
16
17
18
19
camping
revisions
20
21
TURN IN REPORT
22
23
24
25
26
27
28
29
30

Allow ample time in your schedule for rewriting at a deliberate pace. Without time for rereading and some calm thought about how to effect repairs, you will defeat your purpose in writing.

> *I have rewritten—often several times—every word I have ever published. My pencils outlast their erasers.*
> —Vladimir Nabokov

Two-Level Editing

The key to good rewriting is dividing the job into two levels: first-level editing, in which you improve the writing (organization, content, style), and second-level editing, also known as copyediting, in which you correct the language (punctuation, grammar, mechanics).

When you wear both editorial hats—whether you are the author or are editing someone else's writing—it's important that you wear one hat at a time. Focus on one editing level during each reading of the document. If you try to catch errors in grammar while looking for breaks in continuity, you will probably lose track of one or the other. Efficiency in editing comes not from a single, all-purpose reading, but from several readings, each with a different focus.

Put on your first-level editor's hat to look at content and style. It's easier to detect abrupt transitions between paragraphs or poorly supported arguments in the first reading. Flag other problems so that you can find them later—and keep moving. You don't want to get bogged down in minor corrections when you're looking for broad-brush flaws of organization and logic. Save the finishing touches of second-level editing until you've chopped out the underbrush and eliminated the blind alleys. That way you don't waste time punctuating a paragraph you later delete.

Separate readings for certain elements of editing will assure consistency. For example, does the tense of verbs wander between past and present without reason? You can catch such disconcerting lapses more easily if you skim through once looking only at verbs. Are the captions of illustrations and tables parallel in form? If you devote one reading to captions only, you are more likely to notice irregularities.

An Editing Checklist

The following checklist presents a series of questions, designed as a review of the fundamentals of writing and as a way to acquaint you with the contents of this book. How you use the checklist is up to you. If you're an inexperienced writer, you can use it to help corral your material and shape it into the first draft. Once the first draft is completed, going back over the questions will show where you need to revise. Cross-referenced pages in the checklist will lead you to more information about a given subject.

If you are a seasoned writer, you might not refer to the checklist until late in the editing process, and then only to confirm that you haven't overlooked anything. If you need to be prodded about just a few topics, create your own checklist aimed at those weak spots.

The more you work with a checklist, the less you will need it. As you develop your skills, the checklist approach to good writing and editing will become second nature.

An Editing Checklist

FIRST-LEVEL EDITING: *TO IMPROVE WRITING*

LOOK AT THE CONTENT

BIAS:
Have you used slanted words, inappropriate labels, or stereotypes?
Have you given parallel treatment in matters of sex, race, age, and
ability?
> See *Keep Out Bias: Equal Opportunity Writing,* p. 22.

AUDIENCE:
Is the writing directed to a specific reader, or a specific type of reader?
Does the writing match what is known about that audience?
Does the approach take the reader's knowledge into account?

- for a lay audience, are terms defined? examples provided?

- for an audience of experts, have enough facts been presented?

- have conclusions been supported by evidence?

Have examples been used to help the reader understand?
Are answers provided for the questions readers are most likely to
ask?
Does the writing have the right tone? the right amount of formality
or informality?
> See *Write to Your Audience,* p. 34.

LOGIC:
Are the ideas clear?
Was there a plan? Was it followed?
Is the information coherent?
Is it presented according to a logical scheme?
> See *Have a Plan,* p. 38.

INTEREST:
Does it grab the reader?
Does the title enlighten and intrigue?
Are there enough headings?
Does the beginning make the reader want to read on?

Are important points emphasized?

Is there a variety of sentences? sentence lengths? paragraph lengths?

Does the ending provide a sense of completeness?

See *Grab Their Attention*, p. 44.

CLARITY:

Are any words or sentences ambiguous?

Will readers always understand what words like *it* and *they* and *this* refer to?

Will readers be able to follow your train of thought?

Have you used specific rather than vague words?

Do you tell readers what's coming by using words like *but* or *therefore*?

Are all the necessary prepositions there?

Have any double negatives slipped by you?

See *Make It Clear*, p. 54.

CHECK THE STYLE

BREVITY or CONCISENESS:

Have you used too many words?

Are there redundancies? padding?

See *Trim the Lard*, p. 66.

USAGE:

Have you used the right words to convey your meaning?

Are singular and plural words used correctly?

See *Know Your Words*, p. 72.

Have you used overworked expressions?

See *Cut Clichés and Hackneyed Expressions*, p. 77.

Have you used the active voice wherever possible?

Have you avoided lifeless verbs (*to be, exist, occur*)?

Are words unnecessarily hedged with qualifiers (*almost, somewhat, very, little*)?

See *Speak Out*, p. 79.

Does gobbledygook create a verbal smokescreen?

See *Eschew Jargon*, p. 83.

Do your words create the right kind of picture?
Are metaphors used effectively?
See *Use Words Your Readers Can Picture*, p. 85.

Was enough attention paid to small words like *a*, *an*, and *the*?
Have you used contractions correctly (especially *it's* and *there's*)?
See *Be Careful with Small Words*, p. 86.

Did you follow up revisions to see if they affected surrounding
    material?
Did unwanted rhymes or "echoes" appear?
See *Check for Awkward Places*, p. 89.

SECOND-LEVEL EDITING: *TO CORRECT LANGUAGE*

PUNCTUATION:
Do your punctuation marks help the reader grasp the meaning?
Have you removed surplus punctuation?
See *Punctuation*, p. 92.

Do you need help with apostrophes? See p. 92.
    with colons? See p. 96.
    with commas? See p. 98.
    with dashes? See p. 102.
    with ellipses? See p. 103.
    with hyphens? See p. 103.
    with quotation marks? See p. 106.
    with semicolons? See p. 110.

GRAMMAR:
Do subjects and verbs agree?
Do pronouns and antecedents agree?
See *Agreement,* p. 112.

Are pronouns in their correct case (e.g., *who* or *whom*, *I*, *me*, or
    myself)?
Do pronouns refer clearly to their antecedents?
See *Pronouns*, p. 118.

Are adjectives and adverbs used correctly?
Are modifiers correctly placed, close to the words they modify?
Have dangling and misplaced modifiers been removed?
See *Adjectives and Adverbs*, p. 120.

Is the tense and mood of verbs consistent?
　　　　See *Verbs*, p. 123.

Are related parts of sentences or headings parallel in form?
　　　　See *Parallel Structure*, p. 126.

Are sentences complete (i.e., no unintentional fragments)?
Are there any run-ons?
　　　　See *Sentence Faults*, p. 127.

MECHANICS:
Have abbreviations been kept to a minimum? Are they correctly used?
　　　　See *Abbreviations*, p. 130.

Is capitalization correct and consistent?
　　　　See *Capitalization*, p. 137.

Are numbers below 10 spelled out?
Are numbers of 10 and above written as figures?
　　　　See *Numbers*, p. 146.

Are words correctly spelled?
Does the treatment of compounds (as one word, two words, or
　　　hyphenated) make meaning clear?
　　　　See *Spelling*, p. 148.

Have you minimized hyphenation at the right margin?
Are words divided correctly?
　　　　See *Word Division*, p. 158.

Are there any gaps in page numbering?
Have all the tables and figures been included and numbered correctly?
Does the Table of Contents match the text?
　　　　See *Document Integrity*, p. 161.

Is the layout (format) attractive?
Is it easy to read?
　　　　See *Document Appearance*, p. 161.

STYLE SHEET

A B C D		E F G H	
dialogue	53	Federalism	72, 79
bi-lingual	106	_eminence grise_	51
bodacious	12	halftone	43
Breathalyzer	46	freelance	103-5, 110
ad hominem	73	European Common Market	79

I J K L M		N O P Q	
middle-class junkies	66	question-begging generalization	25
machismo	67	the Pentagon	89
lowercase	21, 23, 85	Op-Ed page	66
		palimony	67, 69

R S T U V		W X Y Z	
under way	153	white-collar crime	15
renege	94	win-win situation	12
right-to-die movement	123	X-rated films	34
uppercase	21, 23, 86		

NUMBERS		ACRONYMS, ABBREVIATIONS	
the 20's	72	OPEC	34-7
		IRA	59

Creating a Style Sheet

As you edit, you encounter words that reflect decisions on how certain words are spelled (*esthetic* or *aesthetic*), capitalized (*Federal* or *federal*), and on how compound words are treated (*hand gun*, *hand-gun*, or *handgun*). A style sheet helps you keep track of those decisions so you can be consistent. It's a useful device if you are the only editor—an essential one if two or more are editing the same material.

To make a style sheet, divide a blank page into boxes. Put a few letters of the alphabet at the top of each box. Reserve a box or two for acronyms and numbers. When you come to a place in the manuscript where a style choice has been made, such as spelling or capitalization, write in the appropriate box both the term and page number where it first appears. Thus, *subpoena* would go in the Q,R,S box to show its spelling. *Letter-quality printer* would go in the K,L,M box to show the hyphenation. Refer to the style sheet each time you encounter such items to see how you treated the term before. If you think you might change your mind as you progress, list each page where a term appears to help you find them later for corrections.

If you are editing a particularly long document, you might want separate style sheets for hyphenation, capitalization, and spelling. Another possibility is to put fewer letters in each box, using several sheets to accommodate the whole alphabet.

Proofreading

Proofreading is the last step in the writer's quality assurance program. It consists of comparing the pages produced by the typist or typesetter (the "proof") with the author's final draft in order to confirm that editing changes have actually been made. It also catches new typos and errors that previously escaped notice.

Authors should be the first to proofread their work. But since they often fail to see their own mistakes, it's smart to have another person proofread as well. The best way to proofread important documents is to have two people work together. One person reads aloud from the proof while the other follows along with the author's final draft. The reader should speak clearly and call out beginnings of paragraphs, italics, capitalization, and all punctuation marks. If only one proof-reader is a good speller, have that person be the one reading the proof.

If you don't have a proofreading partner, use rulers to track the lines of type being compared. Try reading backward as well as forward to help you catch doubled words. By slowing you down and obliterating the meaning of the text, reading backwards improves your chance of seeing the actual words, instead of the words your mind tells you are there.

Keep the following questions in mind during proofing.

> Have any words or lines been left out?
> Have all letters or words that were to be deleted actually been removed?
> Have revisions created unacceptable breaks at the end of a line or page?
> Have any typos slipped in?

When you have made one correction in a sentence, re-read the entire sentence. In concentrating on the first error, you may have missed a later one.

Typos that produce legitimate words are hard to catch—and sometimes unintentionally funny. Here are some of my favorites.

> Look for prescription drugs on which the patients have expired.
> The militia went into the countryside, fathering troops.
> Scientists can develop computer programs that stimulate oil reserves.
> The great steal of the State of New Jersey ...
> The copulation statistics reveal a high level of mobility.

Make your corrections bold and clear. On double-spaced typewritten pages, you can enter minor corrections between lines as long as the corrections are legible and understandable. On single-spaced or typeset material, place corrections in the margins. If a change doesn't fit in the margin or between the lines, put it on a slip of paper and attach the paper, properly identified, to the page to be changed. The sticky yellow paper that can be attached and removed repeatedly is ideal for the job; it can also be used as a reminder to verify a statistic or check a reference. Put a major addition on a separate sheet of paper and indicate where it should be inserted.

Run a horizontal line through a word or phrase to be deleted. Run a vertical line through individual letters you want removed. Run a diagonal line through a capital letter you want to make lowercase.

If you change your mind about something you've crossed out, write "stet" in the margin. If you want to restore only part of the crossed-out material, put a dot under each letter you want retained.

If you add punctuation marks directly in the text instead of in the margin, mark them so they won't be overlooked. Circle any periods or hyphens ⊙⊖ ; put carets above commas ⌄ and below quotation marks ⌄, apostrophes ⌄ , and footnote numbers ⌄ .

The proofreader's marks in the chart below are an efficient short-hand; they originated in the printing industry but have been widely adopted. If you use these marks, be sure the person typing the corrected draft understands their meaning. A photocopy of this chart should do the trick.

Proofreader's Marks

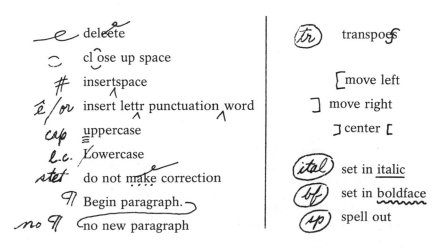

(bf)] A MARKED-UP MANUSCRIPT [

An American, instead of going in a leisure hour
to dance merrily at some place of public resort, as
the fellows of his calling continue to do
throughout the greater part of europe, shuts (cap)
home himself up at to drink.

no ¶ / (sp) He thus enjoys (2) pleasures; he can go on thinking (tr)
of his business, and he can get drunk decently
drunk by his own fireside. . . . ¶ In America I saw
the freest and most enlightened men, placed in the
happiest circumstances which the world affords.
[Yet] it seemed to me as if a cloud habitually hung
upon their brow, and I thought them serious and   #
almost sad even in their pleasures . . . , forever
brooding over advantages they do not possess.
(sp) / l.c. -- (A.) de Tocqueville, _Democracy in America_   (ital)

CORRECTED VERSION

A MARKED-UP MANUSCRIPT

An American, instead of going in a leisure hour to
dance merrily at some place of public resort, as
the fellows of his calling continue to do throughout the greater part of Europe, shuts himself up at
home to drink. He thus enjoys two pleasures; he
can go on thinking of his business, and he can get
decently drunk by his own fireside. . .

In America I saw the freest and most enlightened
men, placed in the happiest circumstances which
the world affords. [Yet] it seemed to me as if a
cloud habitually hung upon their brow, and I
thought them serious and most sad even in their
pleasures . . . , forever brooding over advantages
they do not possess.
--Alexis de Tocqueville, _Democracy in America_

Chapter 3

Keep Out Bias: Equal Opportunity Writing

Chapter 3.
KEEP OUT BIAS:
EQUAL OPPORTUNITY WRITING

Most writers would agree that it's just plain smart to remove bias from writing. After all, the goal is to communicate, and that's hard to do if your words show prejudice that offends readers. Many writers, however, are unaware of the bias in their writing. Furthermore, this subject is complex and involves issues of length (equal time) and topic (equal presentation) as well as word choice, so most of us need help in removing bias.

Look for both the subtle and the not-so-subtle forms of insensitive writing. Offensive stereotypes and obviously slanted words are easy to detect. It's harder to catch bias that reveals itself in uneven treatment or hidden assumptions. The biographical sketch of a professor of biochemistry that describes "Sharon's research in mycotoxins ..." is slanted writing—unless her male colleagues are also given the first-name treatment. When a writer marvels about an older person who plays tennis or jogs, we see a hidden assumption at work: that the rocking chair is the norm for everyone over 60. Such attitudes risk alienating not only those readers affected by the assumption, but also those who notice the slant.

The pressures to remove bias in the areas of sex, race, age, and ability have been considerable in recent years. Although progress has been made, some attempts to comply have produced awkward substitutes. The following paragraphs suggest better solutions for replacing problem words, eliminating biased attitudes, and giving parallel treatment.

REPLACE BIASED WORDS

Biased Words in Areas of Sex

Avoiding sexist terms has been the subject of entire books. Here we focus on three important areas: the word *man*, social titles and salutations (the *Dear Sir* problem), and masculine pronouns used for both sexes.

The emotional, sexual, and psychological stereotyping of females begins when the doctor says "It's a girl."
—Shirley Chisholm

Man. Whether as a prefix (*manpower*), a suffix (*chairman*), or a separate word, *man* evokes a strong reaction in some readers. Since *man* can refer both to a male person and to both sexes, it introduces ambiguity that some readers find unsettling or even offensive. You can usually revise to avoid the word altogether.

Biased: Select a spokesman for your group.

Neutral: Select someone to speak for your group.

You can also find substitutes. Use the following list as a guide in devising your own.

CHANGING SEXIST TERMS

anchorman	anchor
ancient man	our ancestors
businessman	executive, manager, entrepreneur, merchant
chairman	chair
committeeman	committee member (or member of the committee)
common man, man in the street	average person, average voter
congressman	member of Congress
councilman	council member
draftsman	drafter
foreman	supervisor
layman, laymen	layperson, lay audience
layman's terms	non-technical language
longshoreman	dock worker
mailman	letter carrier
man (noun)	human, humanity, human beings, persons, civilization, human race, creatures
man (verb)	staff (as in *staff the booth*) operate, run, work
man-hours	hours, work-hours, staff-hours
manpower	personnel, staff, workers
men	people
newsman	reporter, journalist

repairman	service rep
salesman	salesperson, marketing rep
servicemen	soldiers
spokesman	representative
statesman	diplomat
watchman	guard
workmen	workers

Notice that few of the substitutes include the word *person*. In the swings of action and reaction to the sexism-in-language debate, *person* acquired a mild taint and even became the subject of jokebooks. If there is a workable alternative to *person*, use it. But describing Mr. Doe as *chairman* and Mrs. Doe as *chairperson* is still sexist. Be consistent by using both *chairman* and *chairwoman*, as appropriate, or by using the neutral *chair*.

Some writers insist that their readers will understand that both sexes are included when they use the word *man*. But few readers would consider that both sexes are included if *man* is preceded by or *a* or *the*, as in the following:

> The man who holds the chalk controls the meeting.

You lose nothing and gain much when you remove such bias.

> The one who holds the chalk ...
> The person who holds the chalk ...
> Whoever holds the chalk ...

See how easy it is? Here are some more examples.

Biased: *A serious effort during the period of revision is always called for if the writer is an honest man.*—Stephen White

Neutral: A serious effort during the period of revision is always called for if the writer is honest.

Biased: *A pessimist is a man who looks both ways before crossing a one-way street.*—Laurence J. Peter

Neutral: A pessimist looks both ways before crossing a one-way street. *or*

A pessimist is someone who looks both ways ...

Equal Opportunity Writing does not demand the removal of *man* every time it appears. The word *human* is derived from the Latin *humanus*, meaning human beings, as distinguished from lower animals; *manuscript* and *manufacture* are derived from the Latin word for hand, *manus*. Such words present no problem of ambiguity and thus need not be changed or avoided.

Salutations and Social Titles. The era of "Dear Sir" and "Gentlemen" is behind us. The modern solution to the problem of addressing a letter to unknown persons is to eliminate the salutation. The Simplified Letter format replaces the salutation with a subject line (e.g., RETURN OF DAMAGED GOODS) typed in caps three lines above the text of the letter. The complimentary close (e.g., Sincerely) is omitted, and the writer's name is typed four lines below the text. I prefer the Simplified Letter to the cumbersome *Dear Sir or Madam* or *Ladies and Gentlemen*. It is brisk and efficient—a good tone when you lack the name of an individual to address. Here's an example of a letter written in the Simplified format.

The Downtown Bookstore

500 MARKET STREET, SAN FRANCISCO, CALIFORNIA 94100 • (415) 901-9155

April 15, 1906

Fidelity Fiduciary Fireman's Group
135 Insurance Row
Hartford, Connecticut

CANCELLATION OF POLICY

Please cancel fire insurance policy No. 137-X-3948SR which expires on April 17, 1906. I plan to take out a policy with Tri-State Providential Fireman's Indemnity & Casualty Company because of their low rates and earthquake coverage.

Our coverage with Tri-State will not begin until May 1, 1906. Although this means that our bookstore will be uninsured for a couple of weeks, the fine reputation of the San Francisco Fire Department makes the risk appear to be negligible.

EVERETT E. EVANS, Owner
Downtown Bookstore

If you know a person's name but not sex or marital status, you can use the increasingly popular approach of writing the whole name and omitting the social title (i.e., omitting *Mr.* or *Ms.*)

> Dear Jan Venolia:
> Dear L. V. Aiken:

If name and sex are known, use *Mr.* or *Ms.*

> Dear Mr. Goldman:
> Dear Ms. Reilly:

If you know that a woman prefers *Mrs.* or *Ms.*, use it. But unless you have some reason for distinguishing women by marital status, *Ms.* is the best alternative.

Pronouns. It would be convenient if we had a singular word as neutral as *they* to substitute for the masculine pronouns *he*, *him*, and *his*. Unfortunately, the alternatives suggested so far have serious drawbacks. Synthetic words such as *s/he* or *cos* jolt the reader and divert attention. Alternating between masculine and feminine pronouns is also distracting. Here are some better ways to achieve bias-free writing.

• Write in the second person (you) instead of the third person (he, she).

Biased (third person):
> Each applicant should submit his photograph.

Neutral (second person):
> Enclose your photograph with this application.

Biased: If a student observes any violation of the Honor Code, he should report it to the Dean.

Neutral: If you observe any violation of the Honor Code, report it to the Dean.

• Change from singular to plural.

Biased: Keep the background of your reader in mind so you can gear the information to his level.

Neutral: Keep the background of your readers in mind so you can gear the information to their level.

Biased: *If a child lives with approval, he learns to live with himself.*
—Dorothy Law Nolte
Neutral: If children live with approval, they learn to live with themselves.

• Repeat the noun instead of using a pronoun.

Each communication is a challenge to the writer to present information and ideas directly and forcefully, to help the reader along, and to affect the reader in a chosen way. —Robert Barrass

• Rewrite to eliminate unnecessary pronouns.

Biased: Each applicant must submit his resume.
Neutral: Each applicant must submit a resume.

Biased: The employee is vested in the company profit-sharing plan after he accumulates ...
Neutral: The employee is vested in the company profit-sharing plan after accumulating ...

If none of these alternatives works, *she or he* or *his or her* can be used occasionally.

Biased Words in Areas of Race

Problem words are not limited to sexist terms. The word *minority* when applied to nonwhite groups often reveals a limited or inaccurate perspective. People of color make up the **majority** of the world's population. "Culturally deprived" and "culturally disadvantaged" are sometimes applied to individuals who have a rich cultural heritage, but whose heritage simply differs from the white standard to which it is compared.

Being specific is one way to avoid offensive generalities.

Biased: Children from culturally deprived homes ...
Neutral: Children from homes where reading is not encouraged ...
Children from homes where no English is spoken ...

The word "militant" suggests violence, whereas "activist" implies dedication to a principle. Thus, describing a black person as a militant and a white as an activist may reveal more about the writer's prejudices than about the person being described. Be sensitive to the implications of using colors to describe characteristics: "black deeds" or "a yellow coward."

Biased Words in Areas of Age

Applying word labels to older citizens is another ticklish area. Some in this age group are offended by "senior citizen" and prefer "older person," "elders," "retired people," or simply "seniors." "Elderly" may be appropriate for some, but doesn't fit at the younger end of the group. "Golden oldster" is a bit too cute.

Sometimes labels are unnecessary and less informative than their alternatives.

Weak: Senior citizens will be admitted for half price.
Better: Anyone over 55 will be admitted for half price.

Use a variety of terms, being alert to those your audience might find objectionable.

> The prejudice against the old is overwhelming, but not without its irony. People who are prejudiced never become the source of their attacks: A chauvinist never becomes a woman; a racist never becomes a Black; an anti-Semite never becomes a Jew. And yet we continue with an attitude that the old are inferior. On reaching old age, we may be prejudiced against ourselves!
> —Dr. Alex Comfort

Biased Words in Areas of Ability

As more and more disabled individuals are "mainstreamed," their increased visibility has focused attention on the need for sensitivity to bias in this area. The distinction between "disabled" and "handicapped" is a good place to begin; the terms are not interchangeable. A disability is an impairment that interferes with normal functioning; it can be mental, physical, or emotional. A disability becomes a handicap when the disabled person is prevented from compensating for the disability. Thus, a paraplegic who can compete in wheelchair basketball is handicapped if the building in which the game is played does not have an access ramp.

Avoid referring to "the blind," "the deaf," or "the disabled." Grouping by one characteristic overlooks the other characteristics that make blind, deaf, or disabled people individuals. "People who are blind," "disabled people," or "the person who is deaf" is more sensitive language. Some disabled people are trying to remove the stigma of *dis-* by asking to be called "differently-abled." That's an awkward term, but they have a point.

ELIMINATE PROBLEM ATTITUDES

Your writing may be free of biased terms but still offend some readers if it reveals a biased perspective or contains stereotypes. For example:

Biased: The company picnic will be open to all employees, their wives, and families.

Neutral: The company picnic will be open to all employees, their spouses, and families.

Slang expressions connoting bigotry are obvious and easy to avoid. Not so obvious are the more subtle ways in which our language suggests that the viewpoint of whites is the standard by which everything is to be compared.

Biased: The guidelines are designed to protect the rights of all nonwhite students.

Neutral: The guidelines are designed to protect the rights of students of all racial backgrounds.

Ethnic stereotypes are sometimes hidden. The writer who describes a Spanish-surnamed student as industrious or the Scotsman as generous may be fostering the view that most Latinos are lazy or most

Scots tight-fisted. A patronizing tone can slip in unnoticed. In describing its activities in a largely ethnic community, company literature might say "We're here to *help* you." The same copy for a white community would probably read "We're here to *serve* you."

The popular stereotype of an older person is increasingly at odds with reality. Decrepit, confused, ill-tempered, and unhappy may be adjectives that apply to given individuals, but they present an inaccurate picture of the typical person over 60. Vigorous, cheery, productive, and sensible might be just as applicable. Look for hidden assumptions. If your words suggest that a sharp mind is exceptional, you are implying that senility is the norm. Older people vary in appearance, outlook, and capabilities just as young people do.

GIVE PARALLEL TREATMENT

Avoid mentioning sex, race, disability, or age unless it is pertinent.

Biased: A deaf messenger delivered the package.
Neutral: A messenger delivered the package.

Biased: Margaret Bourke-White was a woman photographer who gained nationwide recognition.
Acceptable: Andrea Johnson was the only female reporter allowed to attend the press conference.

Do not describe a man's professional qualifications and a woman's physical appearance.

Biased: Ed Reed, a distinguished attorney with a long record of community service, and his partner Diane Wells, a good-looking black woman, entered the courtroom.
Neutral: Ed Reed and Diane Wells are distinguished attorneys who have served as unpaid advocates in their communities.

Use comparable language when identifying individuals. A columnist in a national magazine failed to do so when he described the activities in a packing room.

> *A young man planed and sanded the wood ... A girl was fitting a sculpture into a specially made crate.*

If she's a "girl," then he should be a "boy." Or the writer could elevate her to the status of a "young woman."

Uneven	Even
ladies and men	women and men
Roger Evans and Ms. Platt	Roger Evans and Donna Platt
Mr. Evans and Donna	Mr. Evans and Ms. Platt *or*
	Roger and Donna
Ms. Platt and Roger	Donna and Roger *or*
	Ms. Platt and Mr. Evans

Mention race or ethnic background only when pertinent. Would you write "Robert Redford, the popular white actor ... "? Then why write "James Earl Jones, the talented black actor ... "? To identify someone by race suggests a white reference point, implying that everyone who is not white needs to be labeled.

Biased: Thurgood Marshall is a black Supreme Court Justice who has a liberal voting record.

Acceptable: Thurgood Marshall was the first black appointed to the Supreme Court. His liberal voting record....

The most bias-free statement makes no mention of race.

Neutral: Thurgood Marshall has a liberal voting record.

An individual's age should also be indicated only when it's needed to convey information.

Acceptable: The nation's oldest Social Security recipient celebrated his 123rd birthday today.

Physical condition or mental capabilities are appropriately mentioned only if they are pertinent.

Acceptable: Evacuation of the nursing home during the fire was complicated by the frail condition of many of the residents.

Unnecessarily drawing attention to a disability creates artificial barriers, segregating people from each other. As with sex, race, and age, disability is a quality that should be mentioned only when it is germane. Be aware that most disabled people are concerned with what the majority takes for granted: access to buildings and buses, and leading full lives within their schools and communities. If you draw attention to their abilities instead of their disabilities, you help reduce their isolation.

Biased: The paraplegic clerk found the missing document.
Neutral: The clerk found the missing document.

On the other hand, to omit mentioning race or sex when it is an important factor is to swing too far in the opposite direction. If an accomplishment is notable because of a person's age or ability, you should mention that aspect.

Acceptable: The smoke was first detected by John Watkins, a blind student living in the dormitory. His prompt action in reporting the fire saved many lives.

Make your writing reflect sensitivity to both your subject and your reader. This doesn't mean taking all the wit, flavor, and variety out of your writing in order to avoid problems. You can eliminate offensive words and biased assumptions without resorting to clumsy solutions that interrupt the flow of ideas; as you become more aware of the subtle ways that bias creeps into writing, you will find it easier and more natural to use bias-free language.

Chapter 4

First-Level Editing:

Content

Chapter 4.
FIRST-LEVEL EDITING: CONTENT

WRITE TO YOUR AUDIENCE

Writing is only half of communicating; someone must also read and understand what you have written. Your audience may consist of many individuals, none of whom you know. Or you may be writing to a specific individual whom you know well. In either case, what you know about your readers' tastes, interests, and level of sophistication should determine your **approach** to a subject and the **tone** of your writing.

Approach

Have you told your readers everything they need to know? When you're immersed in a subject, it's easy to lose sight of how much background the reader needs to grasp your ideas. Too much detail is boring, too little might confuse. In some cases, it's appropriate to spell out, early on, the type of reader you're addressing.

The typical Operator's Manual that comes with a word processor is a notorious example of writing that is out of touch with the reader. One writer realized that she felt intimidated by her word processor because of its manual. "It's not written in English, it's 300 pages long, and it leaves out crucial information that it assumes you know and has no *right* to assume you know." You've probably had similar experiences when grappling with garbled or skimpy information.

When writing for a lay audience, you must define unfamiliar terms or concepts. Your definition needn't be stiff and formal:

> Caisson disease is a disorder in divers and tunnel workers caused by a too rapid return from high pressure to atmospheric pressure, characterized by pains in the joints, cramps, paralysis, and eventual death unless treated by gradual decompression.

Instead, you might define by the context:

> The divers who were working underwater experienced severe cramps and pains in their joints when they returned to the surface too rapidly. This condition, known as caisson disease or "the bends," was treated by increasing the time allowed for decompression.

or parenthetically:

> The divers returned to the surface gradually in order to avoid "the bends" (severe cramping and pains in their joints).

Analogies and examples, especially ones with human interest, help make the subject matter accessible to a lay audience. Whatever the topic, you need to explain the unknown in terms of the known.

> *When a man sits with a pretty girl for an hour, it seems like a minute. But let him sit on a hot stove for a minute, and it's longer than an hour. That's relativity.*—Albert Einstein

When you write for an audience of experts, your "launch point" is different. Only newly coined terms or those from another discipline require explanation. Expert audiences are hungry for facts. They want to know how much something costs, how big the market is, or whether you can scale up from prototype to mass production. Can they duplicate your experimental results? What applications do those results suggest? You can economize on background information, but don't skimp on details that are essential for understanding.

Are your readers likely to agree or disagree with your viewpoint? If you know your audience is sympathetic, you don't have to sell your ideas. But an unconvinced or antagonistic audience requires different handling. Present your strongest arguments with no waffling. Imagine yourself as the reader; what counter-arguments or questions would you raise? Answer them. Does your answer raise other questions? Answer those, too.

Are recommendations part of your message? If so, present them early. Many readers become impatient with following your thought processes step by step, not knowing your conclusions until the end. They want to know your recommendations up front ("what"), and then how you arrived at them ("why").

Slanted writing will erode your credibility with the reader. Avoid making empty claims (*fantastic results*), applying unfriendly labels (*big business, women's libber, bureaucrat*), or using derogatory words (*fad, carp, spurious*). Back up assertions so that readers don't respond with "So what?" or "Why?"

> *No one can write decently who is distrustful of the reader's intelligence or whose attitude is patronizing.*—E. B. White

Tone

Just as you change your tone of voice in different situations, so should you change the tone of your writing. When you're being interviewed for a job, you use one tone of voice. When you're having lunch with a friend, you use another. Similarly, tone in writing is formal or informal, high pressure or low key, partisan or objective.

Correctly judging your audience will help you select the right tone for your writing. A formal, businesslike tone is appropriate when reporting to a superior or applying for a job. The same tone would seem distant and cold when communicating with colleagues or seeking employees' suggestions. If you want to establish a friendly, informal relationship with your readers, use plenty of first and second person (*I, you*). Make the tone conversational by using contractions (*you're, I've*). Don't be afraid to let your humanity show.

Use the kind of tone you would appreciate if you were the reader. If it's hard for you to develop a relaxed, natural style, try writing as if you were writing a letter to a friend. What words would you choose to express your ideas? They probably have the tone you want.

If your writing is more formal than you like, take a look at your vocabulary. If you use outdated expressions like "It did not escape our attention ... " instead of "We noticed ... ," you sound pompous. Change the following words or phrases to make your writing less stiff and pretentious.

Stuffy Words

Change:	to:
accomplish	do
advise	tell
am in possession of	have
anticipate	expect
application	use (noun)
ascertain	find
by the name of	named
caused injuries to	injured
concerning	about
construct, fabricate	build
cooperate	work with
deem	think
desire	want
disclose	show
endeavor	try
ensuing	following
forward (verb)	send, mail
furnish	give
have need for	need
in lieu of	instead of
in the event that	if
indicate	show
initiate, commence	begin
is of the opinion	believes, thinks
kindly	please
lengthy	long
locate	find
methodology	methods
not too distant future	soon
partially	partly
presently	now
prior to	before
procure	get
pursuant to	following, after, since
render assistance to	help
request	ask

Change:	to:
reveal	show
subsequently	later
sufficient	enough
supply	give, send
terminate	end
transpire	happen, occur
unbeknownst	unknown
utilize	use
was witness to	saw
we would like to ask that	please
with reference to	about

Removing stuffy words from your working vocabulary is generally a good idea. However, this doesn't mean that a casual writing style is suitable in all cases. In a business proposal, for example, you develop the desired formal tone by minimizing contractions (*it is* rather than *it's*) and by using the third person (*they* and *the company* rather than *you, I*).

A tone that is firm, honest, and reasoned fits most situations. Condescension ("As you should have been able to figure out by now ... ") and breezy intimacy ("We all know why that happened ... ") have no place in most writing. Irony and sarcasm backfire in the hands of all but the most skilled writers, leaving the reader confused.

Above all else, be consistent. Whatever tone you're aiming for, maintain it. Lapsing from one to another makes it hard for the reader to develop a clear sense of you and your objectives.

> *You can write about anything, and if you write well enough, even the reader with no intrinsic interest in the subject will become involved.* —Tracy Kidder

HAVE A PLAN

At first, your goal is to get all of your ideas in writing without worrying about how they are linked. If you try to organize the material in your head, you may lose some of your thoughts because you're worrying about where they fit in. Jot the subjects down in any order, regardless of whether they are equally important: main points, minor points, examples, comparisons, background material. Write down whatever comes to mind about the topic.

> *Write freely and as rapidly as possible and throw the whole thing on paper. Never correct or rewrite until the whole thing is down. Rewrite in process is usually found to be an excuse for not going on.* —John Steinbeck

When the "dump" of ideas from your head to the page is complete, take time to organize those thoughts into a logical scheme. In effect, you need to create a map that says to your readers, "We are now at A. We are heading for B. Here's the route I will take to get us there." Without such a plan, information is a jumbled heap of facts or ideas. By establishing a skeleton on which to hang details, you make the information accessible and more easily remembered.

Outlining

Drawing up an outline helps crystallize thoughts and sort out categories. Don't be hamstrung by a formal structure of roman numerals and numbered subtopics. Focus instead on the function of the outline, which is to help you manipulate subjects so as to communicate clearly.

You may find ideas easier to shuffle and rearrange if they are on index cards, one point or example per card. You can then create divisions and subdivisions by moving the cards around until they fall into a logical pattern.

If you are editing a draft that was written from a detailed outline, check it against the outline. Did you stray or make changes that detract from an orderly presentation? Was anything left out?

If you are editing material that was written without the benefit of an outline, you may still want to create one. An outline can help you discover imbalances or discontinuities in poorly organized writing.

Creating an after-the-fact outline is easy whether you write with a word processor, a typewriter, or by hand. Work from a copy of the text you're editing, roughly as follows.

As you re-read each paragraph, identify its topic. Just a few key words will do. If the topic is one of your major points, type it in caps or underline it. Place each subtopic on a new line, with no caps or underlining. If there are sub-subtopics, indent them below the appropriate subtopic. Use separate lines for each new chapter or section; use numbering only if it helps you keep track of your ideas

Next, examine your outline. Stripped to essentials, the logic underlying the organization should be evident. Does the outline reveal an imbalance? A minor point may be blown out of proportion by having too much space or too prominent a place devoted to it. Are there holes in your argument? Answer unanswered questions or respond to potential disagreement with what you've written. Leave no exposed flanks that invite challenge. Have you jumped abruptly from one subject to another? Find ways to connect ideas smoothly so the reader isn't confused by irrelevancies or gaps.

If your outline reveals not just gaps but veritable Grand Canyons, you'd better rethink your plan. Don't be discouraged by such a setback. Most of what you have written can probably still be used, but in a better arrangement. Take the time now to clarify ideas or to make needed connections between thoughts—it will pay big dividends in increased readability.

Organization

The task of organizing ideas falls into two steps: (1) grouping similar subjects, and (2) linking those groups logically. Their arrangement is determined by a third element, format.

Grouping and Labeling. Readers find it difficult to grasp too many packets of information at one time. By combining similar items or ideas under a unifying concept, you give them a handle on the information. You consolidate several bits of data (conscientious self-starter, responsive to company needs, able to write well) into one (why you should get a raise).

Suppose you were asked to evaluate different office copiers. You could group your findings under labels that identify pertinent aspects:

    Major Features (speed, appearance)
    Additional Capabilities (reduction, collation)
    Cost (initial, long-term)
    Maintenance (average time between service calls)
    Warranties (guarantee period, coverage)

Within these categories, you could label specific features as "Advantages" or "Disadvantages." You could also identify which capabilities are important for your office. Your approach depends on your purpose, but grouping and labeling make the information easier to absorb.

> *The first rule of style is to have something to say. The second rule of style is to control yourself when, by chance, you have two things to say; say first one, then the other, not both at the same time.* — George Polya

Linking the Groups. Next, link the groups of ideas according to a logical scheme. The framework that best suits your purpose will take into account your readers' needs and interests and how ideas naturally come together. Here are several approaches to imposing order on writing.

Steps in a process. Describes procedures, step by step, like a recipe.

- Used in instructions, operator's manuals, how-to articles.

Chronological. Traces the sequence of events: what happened and when.

- Used in progress reports, biographical or historical sketches, accident reports, legal depositions, trip reports.

Analytical. Presents data, draws conclusions.

- Used in annual reports, feasibility studies, investment memos, market surveys, consumer reports.

Comparison. Emphasizes similarities and differences or advantages and disadvantages.

- Used in feasibility studies, surveys of competition, product comparisons, building site evaluations.

Geographical. Describes subjects by region.

- Used in market surveys, sales reports, travel articles.

Within such general frameworks, you have still more choices about how to organize your information. For example:

- most to least important (or vice versa)
- least to most controversial
- negative to positive (or vice versa)
- deductive or inductive reasoning
- general to specific

When making a recommendation, it often pays to begin with your most important point. However, "least to most controversial" may be necessary if your readers need to be persuaded. "Negative to positive" will avoid your being charged with dodging issues; it also leaves readers on a positive note.

Typically, several methods of organization are used within one document, possibly within a single paragraph. An annual report, for example, could announce record earnings (most to least important), introduce new products (analytical), describe regional operations (geographical), report on the competition (comparison), and recommend how shareholders vote (least to most controversial).

Make each paragraph a coherent unit with a limited and well-defined purpose. One thought: one paragraph. Use the first sentence (the topic sentence) to tell what the paragraph is about (the thesis); relate subsequent sentences to the thesis. For example:

> *Men make history and not the other way round. [Topic Sentence] In periods where there is no leadership, society stands still. Progress occurs when courageous, skillful leaders seize the opportunity to change things for the better.*—Harry S. Truman

As you edit for logical organization, you may find an idea that's out of place or a major point that's buried in the middle of a paragraph. Rearrange the sentences until the pieces fit together smoothly.

You can reshuffle whole paragraphs with less cut-and-paste if you write each paragraph on a separate piece of paper. Best of all, of course, is the ease of rearranging that comes with writing on a word processor (see Chap. 9).

Format. Format determines the basic structure of your writing. It identifies the main topics and the supporting ideas or information, bringing them together in a unified whole. The format you choose prescribes how the various sections or chapters are differentiated, and the types of headings to be used. It also identifies the conventions of punctuation and mechanics. A clear format suggests that the writer is in charge of the material.

Company policy or an in-house style guide often dictates format. But even when you must work within a prescribed format, you can probably adapt it to your purposes in order to call attention to certain points. Use white space, numerals, headings, and underlining to emphasize key ideas. By efficiently identifying the main points, a good format helps busy readers grasp the basic thrust of your presentation.

If you need help in devising a format, refer to *The Chicago Manual of Style* (see Bibliography). Consistency is the key. It matters less whether headings or lists have periods

1.
2.
3.

or parentheses

(1)
(2)
(3)

than it does that you use the same form throughout.

GRAB THEIR ATTENTION

The attention of your audience may be automatic if you are writing about a topic of interest to them, or if they are obliged to read what you have written. But clear, vigorous writing is both a courtesy and an insurance policy even with a captive audience. It assures that your writing will actually be read.

Titles

The title is your first chance to catch the reader's attention. Is it informative? There should be no question what the subject is, yet the title needn't be dull or wordy. "An Overview of the Structural and Conceptual Characteristics of Future Planning Systems" strikes out on both counts. "Planning: System or Chaos?" might get you to first base.

A short title is easier to remember, so boil it down to as few words as possible, and then play with them a little. Does it help to phrase the title as a question? Perhaps the main title can be the attention grabber and the subtitle can flesh out the subject. Sometimes a play on words is effective, but be careful about being too cute. Notice titles that you come across in your reading. What makes them work—or not work?

Headings

Your next chance to catch the reader's eye is with headings. Headings provide information as well as visual breaks; they reveal the structure of your text, making it easier to locate information or follow the flow of ideas. A busy reader can skim headings to find the sections of most interest.

Compare the appearance of the two memos on pages 46 and 47, one with and one without headings. Which would you pluck from a stack of incoming mail?

●

Headings can be centered, flush left, indented, underlined, or bold-face; they can be all capital letters or upper and lowercase. The text that follows a heading either starts a new line or is run in on the same line as the heading. Establish a pattern to make your headings consistent. Here are two styles to illustrate different treatments.

FIRST ORDER HEADINGS

Second Order Headings
Text follows on next line.
Third Order Headings: Text run in on same line.

FIRST ORDER HEADINGS

Second Order Headings: Text run in on same line.
Third Order Headings: Indented, text run in on same line.

Headings can be single words:
    Introduction
    Analysis
    Conclusions
    Summary

phrases:
    Tracking Regional Performance
    Absenteeism under the Flexitime Program

complete sentences:
    Regional performance is uneven.
    Flexitime reduces absenteeism.

or questions:
    Are regional sales uniform?
    Will Flexitime improve productivity?

Make the style of comparable headings parallel. Use similar verb forms, noun phrases, or complete sentences and keep them in the same order. This helps the reader understand how different sections are related.

Version
A

TO: Agents of Tri-State Providential Fireman's
      Indemnity & Casualty Co.
FROM: Homer S. Pringle, President
SUBJECT: Increasing Our Sales in the San Francisco
      Area
DATE: April 1, 1906

Tri-State Providential has offered fire insurance
to San Francisco businesses for over six decades.
During this interval, many civic-minded individuals
have worked to make the city's fire department one
of the finest in the world. As a result, San
Francisco has been free of conflagration for nearly
55 years.

The increasingly lucrative market in San Francisco
has attracted the attention of insurance companies
around the world, some of whose methods have been
no less than cut-throat. For the first time in our
company's history, we have experienced a decrease
in new business and the loss of some longstanding
customers.

Although we have never before cut prices to attract
and retain business, the present competitive
environment has forced us to reevaluate traditional
practices. Our Board of Directors has concluded
that we must cut prices dramatically if we are to
retain our preeminent position in the California
insurance industry. Please notify your customers
that their fire insurance premiums are reduced by
50 percent, effective immediately. We are certain
that these new rates will help you attract business
while retaining the loyalty of established clients.

We are also aware, however, that it will take more
than lower premiums to meet and eliminate our
competition. The Board is therefore increasing the
coverage provided to all our policyholders, at no
extra cost. Effective April 15, 1906 all holders
of Tri-State fire insurance policies will be fully
covered for earthquake damage.

TO: Agents of Tri-State Providential Fireman's
      Indemnity & Casualty Co.
FROM: Homer S. Pringle, President
SUBJECT: Increasing Our Sales in the San Francisco
      Area
DATE: April 1, 1906

Background
Tri-State Providential has offered fire insurance
to San Francisco businesses for over six decades.
During this interval, many civic-minded individuals
have worked to make the city's fire department one
of the finest in the world. As a result, San
Francisco has been free of conflagration for nearly
55 years.

The Challenge
The increasingly lucrative market in San Francisco
has attracted the attention of insurance companies
around the world, some of whose methods have been
no less than cut-throat. For the first time in our
company's history, we have experienced a decrease
in new business and the loss of some longstanding
customers.

Tri-State's Response
Although we have never before cut prices to attract
and retain business, the present competitive
environment has forced us to reevaluate traditional
practices. Our Board of Directors has concluded
that we must cut prices dramatically if we are to
retain our preeminent position in the California
insurance industry. Please notify your customers
that their fire insurance premiums are reduced by
50 percent, effective immediately. We are certain
that these new rates will help you attract business
while retaining the loyalty of established clients.

Eliminating the Competition
We are also aware, however, that it will take more
than lower premiums to meet and eliminate our
competition. The Board is therefore increasing the
coverage provided to all our policyholders, at no
extra cost. Effective April 15, 1906 all holders
of Tri-State fire insurance policies will be fully
covered for earthquake damage.

Compare the following two groups of headings. The first is a hodge-podge of verbs, nouns, and sentences; the reader would have trouble seeing any relation between them. The second has parallel forms of verbs that clearly present the topic (ways to use a video recorder).

Awkward: Training Technicians
Use Your Recorder to Screen New Employees
Time-and-Motion Studies
How to Improve Quality Control

Parallel: Train Technicians
Screen New Employees
Document Time-and-Motion Studies
Improve Quality Control

A consistent format (e.g., capitalization, underlining) also helps the reader perceive the relation between headings. (See p. 126 for more about parallelism.)

A heading is not the first sentence of a paragraph. Therefore, the sentence that begins a paragraph should be understandable without referring to the heading. For example:

Wrong: *City to Issue Bonds*
They will be a primary source of revenue ...
Right: *City to Issue Bonds*
Tax-free bonds will be a primary source of revenue ...

Openings

Get to the point quickly. Readers want to know what you are writing about and why it's important to them. This doesn't mean beginning with a plodding "The purpose of this memo (report, article) is to ...". An effective beginning incorporates purpose indirectly, perhaps even dramatically.

> Battle lines are being drawn between smokers and non-smokers in offices across the country. Caught in the middle are the companies on whose grounds this war is being waged. How are they coping? This report describes some of their solutions and presents choices for XYZ Company to consider.

Readers know what to expect from such an opening. It states the problem and the scope of what follows.

Jumping right in with your recommendation is another approach.

> Providing separate working areas for smokers and non-smokers is the best way to placate angry employees on both sides of the question. It's a solution that restaurants, airlines—even hotels—and a growing number of companies have adopted.

You leave no question about where you stand with such an opening. Someone who asked for your recommendation or proposal would presumably be receptive to this up-front approach. But if readers disagree with your recommendation, they may read no farther. It's safer to use a recommendation-first opening when you know you have a friendly audience.

Emphasis

Are details supplied in proportion to importance? Check to see if your major thesis is diluted by lesser points. When you know more about a minor point than a major one, you may be tempted to display your knowledge with lots of words. Resist the temptation.

The way you construct sentences also subordinates one idea to another. Moving the transitional words *but* and *although* changes the emphasis in the following sentences.

> The new assembly line has produced some lemons, but genuine progress has been made.

> Genuine progress has been made, although the new assembly line has produced some lemons.

You can emphasize important points in other ways, too.

- Bullets: To make short items stand out

- Underlining: To focus on topic sentences or to stress specific words or phrases

- Capital Letters: To provide a visual break or make a brand name stand out

- Indentations: To set off quotations or bulleted information

- Numbering: To identify groupings

An occasional question-and-answer format draws the reader into your line of thought.

> Is Flexitime the only way to reduce absenteeism? Obviously not.

A colon focuses attention on what follows.

> Leased equipment has one major advantage: flexibility.

The order in which you present items creates emphasis. The beginning is the most prominent place in a sentence or paragraph. But notice how the following sentences have a built-in kicker at the end.

> *There are several good protections against temptation, but the surest is cowardice.* —Mark Twain
>
> *The most exhausting thing in life ... is being insincere.*
> —Anne Morrow Lindbergh
>
> *If you would know the value of money, go and try to borrow some.* —Poor Richard
>
> *Injustice is relatively easy to bear; what stings is justice.*
> —H. L. Mencken

Variety

A series of declarative, subject-verb sentences produces a drone that soon puts readers to sleep.

> Company profits fell 14% during the last quarter. Analysts attributed the decrease to foreign competition. Recovery is anticipated in the coming reporting period. ... (snore)

You can break away from such monotony by varying *sentence structure*, *sentence length*, and *paragraph length*. Some writers do this instinctively, without any linguistic terminology. Others are more comfortable with the following analytical approach.

Varying Sentence Structure. Sentences are classified as *simple, compound*, and *complex*. A *simple sentence* is a subject and predicate (in other words, an independent clause—one that can stand by itself).

> The polls closed at 8 p.m.

A *compound sentence* is two or more independent clauses.

> The polls closed at 8 p.m., and the ballots were counted within an hour.

A *complex sentence* has an independent clause and one or more dependent clauses (a dependent clause cannot stand by itself as a separate sentence).

> Although the polls closed at 8 p.m., we had counted the ballots by 9:00.

As you can see, each type of sentence has a different "personality." Simple sentences are a good device for making short or emphatic statements. Compound sentences work well with two closely related elements or ideas. Complex sentences are good for presenting background information or for subordinating one idea to another.

The following examples show how some eminent people have used all three types. Notice the variety of ways these sentences begin; different beginnings also make writing more interesting.

Simple Sentences:

> *Sacred cows make great hamburger.* —Robert Reisner
>
> *There's no reason to be the richest man in the cemetery. You can't do any business from there.* —Colonel Sanders
>
> *The incestuous relationship between government and big business thrives in the dark.* —Jack Anderson
>
> *Having two bathrooms ruined the capacity to cooperate.* —Margaret Mead
>
> *Brevity is the soul of lingerie.* —Dorothy Parker
>
> *Nothing so needs reforming as other people's habits.* —Mark Twain
>
> *An ounce of hypocrisy is worth a pound of ambition.* —Michael Korda

Compound Sentences:

> *I don't know the key to success, but the key to failure is trying to please everybody.*—Bill Cosby

> *I tape, therefore I am.*—Studs Terkel

> *The cost of living is going up, and the chance of living is going down.*—Flip Wilson

Complex Sentences:

> *Fanaticism consists in redoubling your effort when you have forgotten your aim.*—George Santayana

> *A government is the only known vessel that leaks from the top.*—James Reston

> *If you want a place in the sun, you've got to put up with a few blisters.*—Abigail Van Buren

> *Read over your compositions and, when you meet a passage which you think is particularly fine, strike it out.*
> —Samuel Johnson

> *Show me someone who never gossips, and I'll show you someone who isn't interested in people.*—Barbara Walters

Some sentences don't know when to stop: they just go on and on and...

Varying Sentence Length. If you have varied sentence structure, you have probably varied sentence length. Short sentences are effective for introducing a new subject, long ones for developing a point. Modern writing tends to favor sentences of roughly 20 words. But if a sentence is well crafted and not overloaded with ideas, you can stretch those boundaries with an occasional long sentence. In fact, your writing will be more interesting if you do.

A word processing program that analyzes sentence and word length is useful when editing. It lists average sentence length, length of the shortest and longest sentences, and total number of words, among other things. Using such a program is much easier than counting words yourself and is a good indication of readability.

Varying Paragraph Length. How long are your paragraphs? Generous amounts of white space keep the readers' interest. They also avoid visual monotony and the intimidating nature of solid blocks of type.

Busy people often rely on a quick look at the opening of a paragraph to determine if the rest warrants reading. It follows that more of the document will be read when it consists of short paragraphs. However, lots of one- or two-sentence paragraphs become monotonous and tend to de-emphasize everything on the page. Reserve the shortest paragraphs (even as short as one sentence) for the points you want to stand out.

Closings

> ... *go on till you come to the end; then stop.* —Lewis Carroll

The King's advice to the White Rabbit may seem as useful as Will Rogers' advice to investors: "Buy cheap. When it goes up, sell. If it don't go up, don't buy." How do you *know* when you're at the end? If you have clearly understood your objective in writing, you probably also know when you've achieved that purpose. You will have broken the information into digestible chunks, presented supporting arguments, or provided explanations and examples. In short, because you knew where you were going, you will know when you've arrived.

What remains is to button it up. Are the conclusions you want readers to draw from your evidence clear? Present one last compelling argument to reinforce points you want remembered. In long documents, summarize important ideas in a novel way, rather than simply being repetitious. Where appropriate, indicate the next steps to be taken. Make the ending provide a sense of completeness, so readers aren't left hanging.

Stephen Jay Gould closed an essay on the probability of finding extraterrestrial intelligence with a question.

> *Ultimately, however, I must justify the attempt at such a long shot simply by stating that a positive result would be the most cataclysmic event in our entire intellectual history. Curiosity impels, and makes us human. Might it impel others as well?*

In "The Gift of Wilderness," Wallace Stegner hammers home his message in a long and powerful last sentence.

> *Instead of easing air-pollution controls in order to postpone the education of the automobile industry; instead of opening our forests to greatly increased timber cutting; instead of running our national parks to please and profit the concessionaires; instead of violating our wilderness areas by allowing oil and mineral exploration with rigs and roads and seismic detonations, we might bear in mind what those precious places are: playgrounds, schoolrooms, laboratories, yes, but above all shrines, in which we can learn to know both the natural world and ourselves, and be at least half reconciled to what we see.*

MAKE IT CLEAR

> *Trouble in writing clearly ... reflects troubled thinking, usually an incomplete grasp of the facts or their meaning.*
> —Barbara Tuchman

Clear thinking is a prerequisite for clear writing. However, if your thoughts are a bit muddled when you start to write, the act of writing, itself, may help clarify your thinking. Your real purpose in writing may become obvious only after you have struggled to write down the words and ideas.

Writing is clear when readers can see the point quickly and can follow the supporting arguments. Anything that gets in the way, such as ambiguity or vagueness, is bad writing.

Avoid Ambiguity.

Have you left a reader in doubt as to the meaning of critical words?

Ambiguous: Child killers can be rehabilitated.

"Child killers" could mean people who kill children or killers who are themselves children. Your meaning may be so clear to you that you fail to see the possibility of other interpretations. Here's another example:

Ambiguous: Workshops are limited to assure individual attention and fill up quickly.

Clearly, the person writing that sentence meant that because workshops were limited they fill up quickly. As written, however, classes appear to be limited *in order to* fill up quickly.

> *At first the tendency when reading over one's prose is to find it perfectly lucid and forceful, not to say sublime. This is because the mind that has framed it keeps on supplying its deficiencies from special knowledge and the memory of what was meant.* —Jacques Barzun

Ambiguous: I don't intend to send part of the report.

Does the author of this statement intend to send only the complete report or all but a certain part? Rewrite to avoid such confusion.

Humorists make intentional use of ambiguity.

> *A psychiatrist is a person who owns a couch and charges you for lying on it.* —Edwin Brock

Have you omitted any necessary words? Because too many words have been left out of the following sentences, readers might wonder about their meaning.

> Phil loves power more than his wife.

> San Diego is farther from Los Angeles than Santa Barbara.

Less confusing versions would be:

> Phil loves power more than he loves his wife.   *or*
> Phil loves power more than his wife does.

> San Diego is farther from Los Angeles than Santa Barbara is.

Greta Garbo knew how meaning changes when a word is omitted.

"I never said 'I want to be alone.' I only said 'I want to be *left* alone.'"

Have you omitted punctuation that would help the reader? You will probably have to read the following sentences twice because some necessary commas are missing. Keep your readers moving forward by correcting sentences that demand such backtracking.

After eating the negotiators returned to the bargaining session.

When the headlights are on an indicator light in the pushbutton illuminates the switch.

Since 1980 living standards have dropped 23%.

An omitted hyphen can also be misleading.

Attack Dog Training

The writer of that heading is probably not urging you to forgo Fido's obedience class, but why raise doubts? Add a hyphen, and the confusion disappears.

Attack-Dog Training

(See pp. 103 and 154ff. for more discussion of hyphens.)

Does the position of a word or phrase create ambiguity?

I have discussed how to fill the empty containers with my employees.

The employees might not appreciate such uncertainty as to their disposition. Rewrite:

I have discussed with my employees how to fill the empty containers.

Here's another example:

> In the museum stands a magnificent organ designed by Johann Teitelmann and a 1920 Pierce Arrow.

A remarkable car! Rewrite:

> In the museum stands a 1920 Pierce Arrow and a magnificent organ designed by Johann Teitlemann.

Revise Unclear References

Are your references confusing? When you write *it* or *they* or *her*, will readers know what those pronouns refer to? In general, the reader assumes that a pronoun refers to the noun immediately preceding it. In the following example, however, that assumption would lead the reader astray.

> John Doe is the son of a plumbing supply salesman who died when he was 10.

Who was 10—the salesman or his son? We can make a pretty good guess, but we shouldn't have to. Logic tells us that we must leapfrog back to the word "son" to find the correct antecedent for the pronoun *he.* You can avoid putting readers through such gyrations (and giving them a belly laugh at your expense) by making sure each reference is clear and correct.

Often the best solution is to avoid using a pronoun.

> John Doe, the son of a plumbing supply salesman who died when John was 10, ...

Here are some other examples of unclear references and ways to correct them.

- this, that, these, those

  > Are these words followed by a noun? If not, they are probably faulty references.

  > **Unclear:** The staff has begun analyzing the chain of events that produced the increase in sales. *This* was long overdue.

  This could refer to the analysis or to the increase in sales.

> **Clear:**   The staff has begun analyzing the chain of events that produced the increase in sales. *This* long overdue analysis will shape our marketing strategy ...

- who

> Does *who* refer to the preceding noun?

> **Unclear:**   The chairman of the board, *who* will be available for comment ...

> Will the board or the chairman be available?

> **Clear:**   The board chairman, *who* will be available ...

- it

> Is the word that *it* refers to actually in the sentence?

> **Unclear:**   On the second day the patient's knee was better, and on the third day *it* had completely disappeared.

> The word *it* obviously refers to a physical problem that isn't directly stated in the sentence.

> **Clear:**   On the second day the patient's knee was better, and on the third day the pain had disappeared completely.

- which

> Does an intervening phrase make the reader uncertain of the meaning?

> **Unclear:**   The report of the commission, which attracted so much media attention ...

> Does *which* refer to the commission or the report?

> **Clear:**   The commission's report, *which* attracted ...

Frequently, removing prepositional phrases also removes uncertainty, as the above example illustrates.

Make Logical Comparisons

The bromide about apples and oranges expresses the need to compare similar things. If you are not alert to sentence structure, you may make illogical comparisons. Correcting the illogic often requires no more than one small word, as in the following example.

Illogical: Our company's vacation policy is more liberal than the federal government.

Logical: Our company's vacation policy is more liberal than the federal government's.   *or*

Our company's vacation policy is more liberal than that of the federal government.

Illogical: The Japanese are as strongly motivated as the U.S. and Germany.

Logical: The Japanese are as strongly motivated as Americans and Germans.

Illogical: Dinner here costs no more than any fine restaurant. (An expensive meal!)

Logical: Dinner here costs no more than at any fine restaurant.

Be Specific

Vague words can be misunderstood. "The environment was ameliorated by group effort" could describe a community tree-planting project, an urban redevelopment program, or a tense Board of Directors' meeting.

Vague words also fall short in conveying information. A general statement like "Product X saves you money" is unconvincing. It leaves unanswered the question of "How?". Readers want the specifics: miles per gallon, infrequency of repair, warranties. Writing "She is a good employee" suggests general satisfaction with performance but gives readers no way to confirm that opinion. The more vivid and precise your words, the better the readers will understand and remember them.

Specific: She learns quickly and is eager to increase her skills. When we acquired a word processor, she was the first to master the system. Her help in training the rest of the staff proved invaluable.

Being precise does not require that you be long-winded. One exact word often replaces several inexact ones. Furthermore, precision can be achieved with the plain words that are part of most people's working vocabulary.

Vague	Specific
a better position	a 23% increase in profits
sanitary conditions	safe drinking water
extenuating circumstances	a broken leg
the present writer	I
a plumbing malfunction	a leaky faucet

Examples are a good way to make your writing specific. If you're writing a report weighing the pros and cons of Flexitime, don't stop at citing "improved employee morale" as one of the benefits. Go on to show how.

Employees say they like having time off during the day. They use it for everything from teacher conferences to Christmas shopping. Medical appointments, physical fitness programs, and special events like a concert or ball game are easier to fit into their lives. The majority add that they appreciate just being able to break up the daily routine.

Abstract words can highlight underlying concepts (e.g., productivity, labor relations). But unless you tie down the abstractions with particulars (number of units produced, freedom from strikes), readers have to guess at your meaning. They might despair and decide to do something else rather than fight your prose.

Don't Send Mixed Signals

A poor choice of words can lead the reader first in one direction and then in another. Avoid giving such "false scents."

Confusing: The budget projection was more than $20,000 less than actual income.

Clear: Actual income exceeded the budget projection by more than $20,000.

Use Transitional Words

Certain words tell the reader what to expect. *But* or *however* warns that you're changing direction; *therefore* spotlights a conclusion. Without such transitions, the bridge between sentences is missing, and readers have no time to grasp the full meaning of one idea before the next is thrust upon them.

Confusing: Not all patients do well; some fail completely. The overall results are good.

Clear: Not all patients do well; some fail completely. However, the overall results are good.

Jacques Barzun describes transitional words as the guiding touch to the elbow of someone you are piloting through new sights. Use the following "guiding touches" to pilot your readers.

TRANSITIONAL WORDS

To indicate a conclusion:	thus, accordingly, therefore, so, hence, as a result, consequently
To introduce examples:	for instance, namely, for example, to illustrate
To build a case:	also, similarly, in addition, as well as, furthermore, moreover

To change direction or show contrast	on the other hand, however, on the contrary, even though, nonetheless, conversely, but, yet
To indicate time, place, or order:	finally, first, next, then, further, meanwhile, above all, still, again

Be sure to use these transitions correctly. Don't write "but" unless you actually change direction or show a contrast. Signalling a relationship that doesn't exist is confusing.

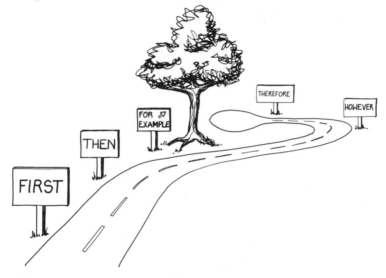

Include All Necessary Prepositions

English idiom requires that we use specific prepositions with certain adjectives or verbs: comply *with,* superior *to,* independent *of.* Omitting any of these prepositions creates an air of incompleteness.

Incomplete: Union members are subject and must comply with the ruling.

Complete: Union members are subject to and must comply with the ruling.

Incomplete: Only one employee knew of the existence or could identify the missing part.

Complete: Only one employee knew of the existence of or could identify the missing part.

If you have doubts about a prepositional idiom, consult a dictionary of idioms or *Words into Type*, which lists 15 pages of them. (See Bibliography.)

Be Positive about Negatives

Multiple negatives create confusion. Readers have to sort them out in order to discover your meaning.

> Snyder did not believe the lack of funding was unimportant.

Just what did Snyder believe? Make your reader's job easier by recasting the negatives in a positive form.

> Snyder believed the lack of funding was important.

If your sentence loses some of its punch when restated positively, find ways to reinject emphasis or drama.

> Snyder believed that the lack of funding could be critical.

Double negatives can be ungrammatical (Don't do nothing illegal) or grammatical (The plan is not without merit). But even grammatical ones may be confusing.

not unaware = aware

Two negatives generally cancel each other. Thus, "I am not unwilling" actually means "I am willing." However, "not unwilling" suggests a slight reluctance—a subtle shading of meaning—that you may occasionally find desirable. Use such double negatives sparingly and only when a positive statement fails to convey your meaning.

> *A not unblack dog was chasing a not unsmall rabbit across a not ungreen field.*—George Orwell

An unintentional doubling of negatives produces a meaning opposite from what the writer had in mind.

> The athlete pursued her goal unrelentlessly.

> *... it's been the lack of just this sort of business contact that's been painfully absent from the Midwestern publishing scene.*
> —from *Publishers Weekly*

When we get into the lack of something being absent, we know we're in trouble. Misplaced negatives are also troublesome.

Misplaced: It is not expected that tomorrow's speech will deal with the economy but will be confined to ...

The expectation is actually there, so the placement of "not" is misleading.

Correct: It is expected that tomorrow's speech will not deal with the economy but will be confined to ...

Review the use of negatives as you edit by looking for "not" and "un-." Is a sentence improved by changing negative to positive? Antonyms are a concise way to make negative statements positive.

> He did not pay attention to the request.
> He ignored the request.
>
> The office will not be open on Labor Day.
> The office will be closed on Labor Day.
>
> They were not present during the interrogation.
> They were absent during the interrogation.
>
> Benzene is not safe to ingest.
> Benzene is highly toxic.

Most words beginning with *in-* are negative:

> ineligible, inappropriate, inaudible.

But some actually have positive meanings and should be used carefully:

> invaluable, inflammable, indebted, inhabitable.

Sometimes double negatives can be fun.

> *If people don't want to come out to the park, nobody's going to stop 'em.* —Yogi Berra

Chapter 5

First-Level Editing:

Style

Chapter 5.
FIRST-LEVEL EDITING: STYLE

TRIM THE LARD

Writers in general use too many words. Those who write with word processors are virtually certain to use too many words. One of the biggest jobs in editing is to prune out those extra words.

As you read each sentence, ask yourself which words could be dropped without changing the meaning. If you have followed the guidelines presented earlier in this book, such as using strong verbs and the active voice, you are well on your way to trimmed-down writing. Removing redundancies and padding should complete the job.

> *There are too many words in prose, and they take up altogether too much room.* —Edwin Arlington Robinson

Redundancies

Is your writing cluttered with groups of words that have the same meaning: *basic fundamentals, separate and distinct, near the vicinity of, exact same, reiterate again, various different,* and *general consensus of opinion?* Not all redundancies are so blatant. "In addition to ... also" and "estimated at about ... " are common ways of covering the same ground twice. Here are some others.

Redundant: The average postal worker's salary, according to their union, averaged $23,592.

Correct: The average postal worker's salary, according to their union, is $23,592.   *or*
Postal workers' salaries average $23,592, according to their union.

Redundant: The age of this tree is more than 1000 years old.

Correct: The age of this tree is more than 1000 years.   *or*
This tree is more than 1000 years old.

Redundant: Some of those arrested included students.
Correct: Some of those arrested were students.   *or*
               Those arrested included students.

Redundant: His remarks were limited only to ...
Correct: His remarks were limited to ...

Redundant: An additional title was added to the list.
Correct: Another title was added to the list.

Redundant: The reason I am late is because my car wouldn't start.
Correct: The reason I am late is that my car wouldn't start.   *or*
               I am late because my car wouldn't start.

~~finally~~ concluded

commute to ~~and from~~

refer ~~back~~ to

a new ~~all-time record~~ high

Some expressions, in addition to being repetitious, reveal a lack of thought. An "unsubstantiated rumor" suggests there could be a substantiated rumor. Writing "your own autobiography"—could you write anyone else's autobiography? Such redundancies are a sign that you're on Auto Pilot and have let unnecessary words or phrases slip through.

The following redundant expressions are grouped by grammatical form. Trim your writing by deleting the parts that are italicized. In the case of *Repetitive Phrases,* delete one part (e.g., either *exact* or *same*).

Redundant Expressions

Adjectives

absolute necessity
active consideration
advance reservation
baffling enigma
both alike
close proximity
complete monopoly
conclusive proof
end result
equal halves
final outcome
free gift
future occurrence
general rule
invited guest
mutual cooperation
new innovation
new recruit
old adage
past history
personal opinion
positive identification
proposed plan
root cause
self-confessed
single unit
surrounding
    circumstances
temporary reprieve
temporary loan
unsubstantiated rumor
usual custom

Nouns

Capitol *building*
component *parts*
doctorate *degree*
weather *conditions*

Prepositional Phrases

green *in color*
brief *in duration*
classified *into groups*
depreciated *in value*
estimated *at about*
few *in number*
filled *to capacity*
large *in size*
last *of all*
plan *in advance*
rectangular *in shape*
smile *on his face*
1 a.m. *in the morning*

Repetitive Phrases

any and all
exact same
if and when
unless and until
just exactly
new all-time record high
today's modern
    manager

Adverbs

completely surround
eliminate *entirely*
might *possibly*
more superior (or
    preferable)
mutually agreeable
really dangerous

Prefixes, Suffixes

*ir*regardless
to the west*ward*
*un*relentlessly

Verb Tails

assemble *together*
attached *hereto*
cancel *out*
connect *up*
continue *on*
enclosed *herein*
face *up to*
follow *after*
hurry *up*
joined *together*
lift *up*
made *out* of
merge *together*
penetrate into
study up
termed as
visit with

Padding

Make each word carry its own weight. "There is room in the basic unit for up to two disk drives" conveys no more than "The basic unit can hold two disk drives," but it is padded with five extra words. "As of now we have no progress to report" starts with three clutter words.

Tightening windy expressions saves on printing and postage, reduces reading time, and improves the likelihood that the document will actually be read. Here are some ways to streamline language by revising or deleting wordiness.

Tighten These

Change:	to:
a large (small) number of	many, few
ahead of schedule	early
along the lines of	like
at a later date	later
both together	together
conduct an investigation	investigate
destroyed by fire	burned
draw to your attention	show, point out
during the course of	during, while
during the time that	while
from the viewpoint of	as (or rewrite)
give rise to	cause
had occasion to be	was
have need for	need
in advance of	before
in connection with	about
in excess of	exceed(s)
in regard (relation) to	about
in the neighborhood of	near, about
make use of	use
not in a position to	unable to, cannot
of such difficulty	so difficult
on a theoretical level	in theory
on a regular basis	regularly

Change:	to:
on two separate occasions	twice
placed under arrest	arrested
proceeded to take	took
put in an appearance	appeared
retain position as	remain
seldom ever	seldom
succeed in making	make
such time as	when
take into consideration	consider
the majority of	most
until such time as	until

Delete These

As far as _____ is concerned
as a matter of fact
as such
for the sake of
in the case of
in some instances
needless to say
said (as in "said device")
take this opportunity
the fact that
the ... mark (as in "The Dow Jones topped the 2000 mark")
the reason is

Watch for These

Although *as to* is useful when introducing a new subject (As to the crew's record of quality control ...), you should question its other uses. You can usually replace *as to* with a better word:

Poor: Applicants were screened as to age and sex.
Better: Applicants were screened by age and sex.

or delete it:

Poor: She expressed doubt as to their ability to meet the quota.
Better: She doubted whether they could meet the quota.

Sentences built along the following lines are cluttered with too many words.

the ... of

> The manufacture of paint is ...
> Paint manufacture is ...
>
> The level of crime ...
> The crime level ...

there ... who/that

> There are some circumstances that require ...
> Some circumstances require ...

it

> It was the Personnel Manager who issued the pink slips.
> The Personnel Manager issued the pink slips.
>
> It seems that Karen is late.
> Karen is late.
>
> It is necessary to sign ...
> You need to (or must) sign ...

but ... nevertheless

> Our account balance is low, but we will meet the payroll nevertheless.
> Our account balance is low; we will meet the payroll nevertheless.   *or*
> Our account balance is low, but we will meet the payroll.

Sometimes removing surplus words forces you to think about exactly what you want to say. Replacing deleted words with others that express your ideas more accurately may make total word count go up instead of down. That's all right. The goal is not simply to lop off words but to make all of them work for you. In practicing an economy of words, you don't want to use so few that the ideas are unclear.

> *I believe more in the scissors than I do in the pencil.*
> —Truman Capote

KNOW YOUR WORDS

The almost-right word is not good enough. "Deprecate" won't do if you mean "depreciate" or "pre-emptory" if you mean "peremptory." A spelling reference, such as *20,000 Words* or the dictionary that comes with a word processor, can help you spell correctly, but it won't keep you from using the wrong word. Make a habit of looking up meanings in a good dictionary. Read respected authors to develop a feeling for the correct use of words.

Ordinary words used precisely are more impressive than big words used sloppily. But even ordinary words can be used imprecisely. Do you write "always" when you should write "usually," "never" when "seldom" is more accurate, or "exactly" when "nearly" is more appropriate?

If you can't decide which of several words to use, put the alternatives in brackets. Later, return to the bracketed spot. The choice may be easier when some time has elapsed—or when you've looked up the meanings of the words.

> *For your born writer, nothing is so healing as the realization that he has come upon the right word.*—Catherine Drinker Bowen

Commonly Misused Words

affect
: Spelling errors with *affect* and *effect* often lead to use of the wrong word. *Affect* is primarily a verb, meaning to have an influence upon (How did the pills affect you?). *Effect* as a noun means result or consequence (The effect of the pills was easy to see.); as a verb, it means to bring about (The pills effected a cure.).

aggravate
: To make worse; not a substitute for *irritate* or *annoy.*

anxious
: Uneasy, apprehensive. Appropriate where apprehension or concern is implied; *eager* is the word to describe earnestly desiring something.

balance
: Appropriate with money; otherwise, use *remainder.*
  Wrong: The balance of your time is your own.
  Right: The remainder of your time is your own.

claim
: Many careful writers prefer the verbs *assert* or *maintain.*

complement
: The verb *complement,* meaning to go well with or satisfy a need, is often confused with the verb *compliment,* meaning to praise.

comprise
: To include or be composed of; avoid *comprised of.*
  The whole comprises the parts. The parts constitute the whole.

criteria
: Plural form of the word *criterion.* Requires a plural verb. (See p. 76.)

dilemma
: Use *dilemma* to indicate two choices, each undesirable. To describe a generally difficult situation, use *predicament.*

effect
: See *affect.*

equally
: Use only where equality pertains.
  Wrong: The night shift performs equally as well as the day shift. (To correct the sentence, delete *equally.*)
  Right: The sum was divided equally among the heirs.

farther	Use with physical distance. (He can see farther than I can.) To indicate extent or degree, use *further*. (Let's study the results further.)
fewer/less	Use *fewer* when referring to individual numbers or units; use *less* when referring to quantity. (Fewer mistakes, less embarrassment.)
fulsome	Means disgusting, excessive, insincere. Don't reach for this word when you mean plentiful.
generally	Is *usually* the word you want?
irregardless	Use *regardless* or *irrespective*, not this bastard mixture of the two.
it's	*It is* or *it has*. The possessive form is *its*. (See p. 89.)
like	Use with nouns or pronouns (She is tall, like her father). Use *as* with phrases (Profits rose, as in the previous quarter).
literally	Means really or actually; don't use as an intensifier. **Wrong:** He literally exploded when he heard the news. **Right:** *There are people in the world who literally do not know how to boil water.*—Craig Claiborne
mitigate	A verb meaning to alleviate or moderate; often confused with *militate*, which means to have force as evidence. Memories of a happy childhood mitigated her grief. Our results militate against continuing the experiment.
percentage	Avoid using as a substitute for *some*.
preventive	Not *preventative*.
principal	An adjective meaning chief or main; a noun designating a school official or, in a legal context, an important person. Often confused with *principle*, which refers to a rule or fundamental truth.

refute	Use in the sense of proving falsity or error; not a synonym for *deny* or *repudiate*.
respectively	Singly, in the order stated. The correct word in the complimentary close of a letter is *respectfully*.
-self	Correct if adding emphasis (I saw the Pope himself) or as a reflexive pronoun (She hurt herself). Not interchangeable with a pronoun. Thus, Stan and I (not Stan and myself) are heading the team.
suspicion	A noun, not a verb. You have a suspicion, or you suspect something, but you don't suspicion something.
that/which	Use *that* to introduce a restrictive clause and *which* to introduce a nonrestrictive or parenthetical one. **Right:** *Your manuscript is both good and original; but the part that is good is not original, and the part that is original is not good.* —Samuel Johnson **Right:** My decision, *which* didn't come easily, is final.
unique	An overworked word, often misused for *rare* or *notable*.

"My dear, a rich vocabulary is the true hallmark of every intellectual person. Here now"—she burrowed into the mess on her bedside table and brought forth another pad and pencil—"every time I say a word, or you hear a word you don't understand, write it down and I'll tell you what it means. Then you can memorize it and soon you'll have a decent vocabulary. Oh, the adventure of molding a little new life!" She made another sweeping gesture that somehow went wrong because she knocked over the coffeepot and I immediately wrote down six new words which Auntie Mame said to scratch out and forget about.
—Patrick Dennis

Incorrect meanings are only one source of error with words. Incorrect plurals are another. Words that come from Latin (*data, criteria, phenomena, media*) are frequently the culprits. Such words have irregular singular and plural forms: *phenomenon* (singular) and *phenomena* (plural). Since the words are not made plural by adding *s* or *es*, as is customary with words like *chair* or *box,* many people don't know whether they are using a singular or plural word. They make two kinds of mistakes:

(1) Using the plural form of the word when singular is called for.

> Age was the sole criteria for determining eligibility.
> (Make that *criterion.*)

(2) Using a singular verb with a plural form of the word.

> The media was excluded from the meeting.
> (Make that *were.*)

Add professional polish to your writing by using singular and plural words correctly. Refer to the following list for help.

Irregular Plurals

Singular	Plural
alga	algae
alumna (fem.), alumnus (masc.)	alumnae (fem.), alumni (masc., both)
analysis	analyses
antenna	antennas (radio, TV); antennae (insects)
apparatus	apparatus
appendix	appendixes
automaton	automatons *or* automata
bacterium	bacteria
consensus	consensuses
crisis	crises
criterion	criteria
curriculum	curriculums *or* curricula
datum	data
formula	formulas
genus	genera

index	indexes (publishing); indices (math)
kibbutz	kibbutzim
matrix	matrices
medium	media
millenium	millenia
phenomenon	phenomena
prospectus	prospectuses
radius	radii
stratum	strata
symposium	symposia
synopsis	synopses
vertebra	vertebrae

matrix + matrix = matrices

CUT CLICHÉS AND HACKNEYED EXPRESSIONS

Words that are overworked lose their force. When every event is described as a "crisis," it's hard to get worked up about another one. We have had a vogue of "gaps," credibility, gender, and generation. Voguish words are a poor vehicle for fresh ideas, so be wary of expressions that seem to appear, unbeckoned, in your mind.

> *Modern writing at its worst ... consists in gumming together long strips of words which have already been set in order by someone else and making the results presentable by sheer humbug.*—George Orwell

If an expression is both hackneyed *and* garbled, you are vulnerable to smirks or outright guffaws.

> Keep a stiff upper hand.
> Opening up a whole can of wax ...
> Chafing at the bit ...
> It created a human cry.
> They just shrugged their noses.
> He's a ragged individualist.

By avoiding clichés altogether, you will appear more professional and will eliminate the chance of misusing them. The expressions on the following list should be avoided.

Overworked Expressions

abreast of the times
add insult to injury
all things considered
along these lines
ample opportunity
as a matter of fact
at a loss for words
at long last
back burner
benefit of the doubt
better late than never
bitter end
bone of contention
by the same token
capacity crowd
chain reaction
checkered career
circumstances over which
   I have no control
city fathers
considered opinion
conspicuous by its absence
controlling factor
crying need
curiously enough
dramatic new move
drastic action
due consideration
eminently successful
equal to the occasion
exception that proves the rule
exercise in futility
existing conditions
festive occasion
few well-chosen words
finishing touches
food for thought
force of circumstances

foregone conclusion
generation gap
give the green light to
grave concern
heated argument
herculean efforts
inflationary spiral
in no uncertain terms
in short supply
in this day and age
iron out the difficulty
irreparable loss
it goes without saying
just desserts
keep options open
last analysis
leaves much to be desired
leave well enough alone
leave no stone unturned
lend a helping hand
line of least resistance
long-felt need
marked contrast
moment of truth
more than meets the eye
narrow escape
needs no introduction
one and the same
on more than one occasion
on unimpeachable authority
open secret
other things being equal
overwhelming odds
own worst enemy
paramount importance
part and parcel
peer group
pros and cons

regrettable incident
reliable source
remedy the situation
ripe old age
round of applause
second to none
select few
sweeping changes
too numerous to mention

unprecedented situation
untimely end
viable alternative
view with alarm
wave of the future
weaker sex
whole new ball game
wide open spaces

SPEAK OUT

Strive for assertive writing. It is direct and crisp, unburdened by the passive voice, lifeless verbs, and too many qualifiers.

Use the Active Voice

When you write in the passive voice, the subject is acted *upon*.

Passive: Joe was hired by Tom.

The voice is active if the subject of the sentence is the "doer."

Active: Tom hired Joe.

The passive voice combines a form of the verb *to be* with the past participle of another verb: *was submitted, are seen, is urged, were reported, has been completed.*

Passive and active voices each have legitimate uses. The passive voice is appropriate in the following circumstances:

• in technical writing

   The air is heated by being circulated over the coils.

• if the object of the action is more important than the subject

   The meeting was postponed.
   The veteran was awarded the Medal of Honor.

• if the subject is unknown

   The article was unsigned.
   Information was leaked to the press.
   Documents were stolen from the secured area.

• when you want to avoid naming a specific person

> The missing papers were returned.
> The time it takes to write a report is wasted if the report is not read.

However, the active voice should predominate in writing. Unfortunately, the passive voice tends to invade all writing and smother it with anonymity. No one does anything—they just have things done to them.

Notice how changing from passive to active voice makes shorter, livelier sentences.

Passive: It is recommended that special attention be paid to how productivity can be improved by introducing profit-sharing.

Who recommends, pays attention, and improves? We have to guess.

Active: Management should consider how profit-sharing can improve productivity.

Passive: They were not notified of the incident.
Active: No one notified them of the incident.

Don't shift from active to passive voice mid-sentence.

Poor: Such a program costs little, and many are benefitted by it.
Better: Such a program costs little and benefits many.

Ferret out passive constructions by looking for forms of the verb *to be*:

> is, am, are, was, were, be, been, being

Replace them with the active voice whenever you can; retain the passive only when the active voice is clearly inappropriate.

Avoid Lifeless Verbs

Lifeless verbs bring the motion of a sentence to a standstill. *Exist, occur,* and forms of *to be* and *to have* are the worst offenders.

Poor: The Neighborhood Watch program exists in certain communities where there is concern about the crime rate.
Better: The Neighborhood Watch program reflects community concern about the crime rate.

It may seem strange to carp at the use of so essential a verb as *to be*. But sentences built on *to be* are frequently heavy with accompanying baggage.

> The purpose of the report **is** to provide a means of comparing sales in the four regions.
>
> The report compares sales in the four regions.
>
> Cutting government spending **is** another way to reduce the deficit.
>
> Cutting government spending also reduces the deficit.
>
> His version **is** significantly different.
>
> His version differs significantly.

Lifeless verbs often reveal excessive use of nouns. When *indicates*, *believes*, and *knows* become *is an indication of, has a belief in*, and *has a knowledge of*, the pace slows down. If you suspect your writing is noun-heavy, look for word endings like *-ment, -tion, -ity, -ance*, and *-ness*. Replace nouns and lifeless verbs along the following lines.

Change:	**to:**
a preference for	prefer
present suggestions for avoiding	suggest ways to avoid
There is a belief among the reporters	The reporters believe
Their response was an indication of	Their response indicated
has a tendency to	tends to

> *What is wrong with most writing today is its flaccidity, its lack of pleasure in the manipulation of sounds and phrases. The written word is becoming inert.* —Anthony Burgess

Don't Overqualify

Too many qualifiers weaken writing. E. B. White dramatically described such words as *rather, very, little,* and *pretty* as "leeches that infest the pond of prose, sucking the blood of words." No hedging there!

Omit qualifiers that diminish your ideas or are inherently contradictory:

rather important	almost unique
more perfect	very fatal
somewhat irresponsible	moderately exhaustive

Replace qualifiers that simply intensify meaning with words that are themselves emphatic:

very important = critical, crucial, central
really angry   = outraged, furious

or just delete them:

very obstinate = obstinate
utterly reject   = reject
very ecstatic   = ecstatic

Review *very* and any qualifiers that have become clichés (*richly deserved, ample opportunity, bitter end*). Replace or delete those that weaken your writing.

ESCHEW JARGON

One definition of jargon is "the specialized or technical language of a particular science or trade." Jargon of this kind has its proper place. It is an efficient shorthand when writing for an audience that understands the terms and special meaning.

But some writers use pseudo-technical words or style simply to impress the reader or to create a verbal smokescreen. People call such jibberish "gobbledygook" and label it with the suffix -*ese*: governmentalese, legalese, educationese. Yet its pretentious and downright dull prose remains an epidemic.

What are the symptoms of gobbledygook?

• A murky **passive voice** predominates. We find neither subject nor actor, just the action: conclusions are reached, relations are improved, and problems are anticipated. (See p. 79.)

• **Prepositional phrases**, unending and uninteresting, often provide the framework of a gobbledygook sentence.

The root *of* the problem *of* negotiation, *in* which there is the interaction *of* representatives *of* groups *with* conflicting points *of* view, is the taking *of* adversarial positions *from* which retreat is difficult.

In any company *with* a mobile sales force, the difficulty *of* coordination *of* input *from* marketing *with* R&D is a challenge *of* the ability *of* management to respond *to* the marketplace.

• **Piled-up nouns** proliferate.

systems modification effort
employee productivity improvement possibilities
highway litter reduction program
damage situation
disabled student learning environment

• **Parts of speech are converted** into other parts of speech. Verbs become nouns:

America is on the improve.

Even more often, nouns become verbs:

> The design was prototyped into a working model.

> We're going to incentivize these people by multiyearing their program.

It appears there isn't a noun that can't be verbed!

• **Abstractions and empty terms** disguise real meaning. Under the mistaken impression that obscureness is profound and complexity has clout, writers stifle their natural style. They don't write "We tested it and it works," but "During the course of the above referenced investigation, data were developed and subjected to rigorous computer modeling which suggest that the system will, within specified parameters, produce viable results."

The first step in getting readers to pay attention to what we're writing is to pay attention ourselves. Too often we regurgitate phrases without having digested their meaning ("decisional significance"). We use high-sounding words for the sake of being high-sounding; an "intermodal interface" means that a bus is waiting when you get off the train, and a "wood interdental stimulator" is a toothpick.

High-sounding terms are sometimes a way to avoid being direct. In this way, what used to be listed on hot dog packages as powdered bone is now called calcium, and the clear-cutting of thousands of acres of trees becomes vegetation manipulation.

> The income derived from the revenue enhancement program will be allocated to revitalizing the nation's infrastructure.

Translation: The gasoline tax will pay for repairing our highways and sewer systems.

> *A good catchword can obscure analysis for fifty years.*
> —Wendell L. Wilkie

• **Buzz words** abound. Many are legitimate words that overuse has turned into clichés (viable, image, dialogue, disseminate, implement, relate). Some are legitimate words in certain contexts but their popular usage tends to be

incorrect (parameter, modality, metaphor, phenomenon). Some have no claim to legitimacy (finalize, learning experience, out years, shortfall, throughput, taxwise).

English is a remarkably clear, flexible, and useful language. We should use it in all of our communications. —Daniel O'Neal, Jr.

USE WORDS YOUR READERS CAN PICTURE

Words, when well chosen, have so great a force in them that a description often gives us more lively ideas than the sight of things themselves. —Joseph Addison

Our language is rich with words that evoke images.

domino theory	the big bang
sticky situation	bamboo curtain
bottleneck	grass-roots campaign

These words appeal to the senses; they help the reader visualize and remember. Yet writers are sometimes unconscious of the imagery they are using. When their images collide or reveal fuzzy thinking, they run into trouble.

His weak knee was his Achilles' heel.

This field of research is so virginal that no human eye has ever set foot in it. —(found in a Ph.D. dissertation)

Keep your images under control. The more aware you are of the pictures words make, the better you will use them. Here's how a master does it.

Sending men to that Army is like shoveling fleas across a barnyard—not half of them get there. —Abraham Lincoln

Metaphors are a technique for creating images. Unlike Lincoln's simile above, which makes a comparison using the word *like*, metaphors establish an identity without such words.

> *Bureaucracy is a giant mechanism operated by pygmies.*
> —Honore de Balzac

When politicians demand that all the fat be cut from the budget, they are creating an identity: the budget *is* an obese organism. Their opponents extend the metaphor by responding that all the fat has been squeezed out and bone is now being cut. In both cases, they say something *is* something else in order to dramatize a point.

> *We are all on a spaceship and that spaceship is Earth. Four billion passengers—and no skipper.*—Wernher von Braun

A good metaphor is transparent; it enhances meaning without drawing attention to itself. A heavy-handed metaphor, or one that contains conflicting images, distracts the reader from the writer's ideas. Use figures of speech, such as metaphors, sparingly. In small doses, they are an artful device, but overuse diminishes their effectiveness.

BE CAREFUL WITH SMALL WORDS

Small words can create big problems if they are misused. Check whether you have used the following small words correctly.

a, an, and the

Incorrect use of the articles *a* and *the* can alter meaning. Notice the difference when *the* is omitted.

> The more specific details you provide ...
> The more specific the details you provide ...

The first emphasizes the quantity of specific details; the second, how specific those details are. Either could be correct. But you must be alert to the nuances of each to choose the one that's closer to your meaning.

Omitting *the* often produces a truncated style of writing that is best reserved for headlines.

> Results of the investigation were announced. (The results ...)

> Joe Turner requested a leave of absence on advice of his doctor. (... on the advice of ...)

Know when each article is called for. *A* is general, one from a large group (Dick is a neighbor). *The* is specific, identifying which one

(Dick is the neighbor who is lending me a car). *The* is mandatory when later words define or identify, as in "the ... of" constructions.

the help of a friend	the will of the people
the formation of a board of inquiry	the turn of the century

The beginning *sound* of the next word determines whether you use *a* or *an*. A consonant sound (which is not necessarily a consonant) is preceded by *a*, a vowel sound by *an*.

a uniform	but	an unprecedented
a European	but	an Easterner
a history	but	an hour
a one-dollar bill	but	an only child

Uniform and *European* are pronounced as if they began with the letter *y*, so *a* is the correct article to use with them. The *h* in *history* is pronounced, so it requires *a*. The *h* in *hour* is silent, calling for *an*. *One* is pronounced as if it begins with *w*.

The choice of the article to precede initials and acronyms is a trap for unwary writers. Again, it is how the acronym or first letter is pronounced that matters. Are the letters pronounced individually (an SEC lawyer, an NBA player) or as a word (a SAC bomber, a NASA official)? Pronounce the initial or acronym to determine if you should use *a* or *an*.

like, as

Use *like* in direct comparisons of nouns (or their equivalent).

> *Hell hath no fury like a bureaucrat scorned.* —Milton Friedman

> *Nothing recedes like success.* —Walter Winchell

> *Having the critics praise you is like having the hangman say you've got a pretty neck.* —Eli Wallich

Use *as* when the comparison involves verbs.

> Do as I do.

> They were late, just as she was.

> He resented the implication, as anyone would.

> *To succeed it is necessary to accept the world as it is and rise above it.* —Michael Korda

with

The American Heritage Dictionary lists 28 uses of the word *with*. Many of them are merely a sloppy way of attaching an additional thought to a sentence, as in these examples.

> The students, with ages ranging from 18 to 22 ...

> The 2001 series will be replaced by the improved 4001 series, with the transition to the newer model occurring next year.

> Test panel members ranked taste and texture as most important, with color a close third.

Rewrite along these lines:

> The students, whose ages range from 18 to 22 ...

> The improved 4001 series will replace the 2001 series next year.

> Test panel members ranked taste and texture as most important; color was a close third.

Review each use of *with*. Is the word overused? Rewrite those sentences where *with* reveals careless writing or woolly thinking.

etc.

Relying on *etc.* at the end of a list suggests that you are either lazy or uncertain about what else should be included. Indicate incompleteness by writing *such as* (or *such ... as*) ahead of examples.

> A well-stocked library will include such authors as ...
> The event produced additional sources of income, such as ...

's

Errors of agreement are common with the contraction *'s*. In fact, such errors are so common that it's probably smart to scrutinize each use of the apostrophe. *It's, there's, here's,* and *that's* are ALWAYS contractions, usually of the word *is*: *it is, there is, here is,* and *that is.* The word *is* is singular. Most people know this, yet they make the mistake of treating the contraction of *is* as a plural. For example, a school principal wrote "I've learned 100 things **that's** good about computers in education." I'm sure she wouldn't write "...100 things that **is** good about computers," but in its contracted form, the combination of plural subject and singular verb escaped notice. (See Agreement, p. 112.)

It's is probably the most misused word in American writing. Since the apostrophe is one way to show possession, it may seem logical to use one when making the word *it* possessive. But *its* is the correct possessive form, and *it's* is a contraction of *it is* or *it has.* Make sure that *it's* is indeed a contraction wherever it appears.

It's a question that suggests its answer.

it's = it is

CHECK FOR AWKWARD PLACES

In the heat of creation, you may not notice that three consecutive sentences begin with the same word or that you have overworked certain expressions. An editor of a major newspaper failed to catch the repeated use of the word *call* in the following paragraph.

> "...what some might call a design counterculture. An abundance of native stones ... were put to good use in what architecture historians are now calling native or vernacular architecture. These granite rocks, sometimes called Claremont potatoes ..."

Has an unintended rhyme crept in? Do some words have echoes? Are sounds repeated? Remove such distractions.

Change:	to:
a selection from the collection	a selection from the portfolio
our products are produced	our products are made
discard cards	remove (or throw away) cards
except for rare exceptions	with rare exception

Sentences that had been logical in their original context can become confusing if they aren't adequately blended into their surroundings when moved. Readers should be unable to detect amputations or grafts; your surgery should leave no scars.

> *A good style should show no sign of effort. What is written should seem like a happy accident.* —W. Somerset Maugham

Chapter 6

Second-Level Editing:

Punctuation

Chapter 6.
SECOND-LEVEL EDITING: PUNCTUATION

This chapter focuses on commonly misused punctuation marks. Wherever possible, punctuation rules are approached via examples rather than academic jargon. However, some linguistic terminology is hard to avoid: participle, nonrestrictive clause, gerund. Rather than clutter a rule with definitions, I have included these terms in a glossary at the end of the book. In many cases you will be able to deduce the meaning of an unfamiliar term from the examples that illustrate each rule.

If you have a word processor, you can use it to locate and correct certain punctuation errors. For example, suppose you have consistently placed final periods outside quotation marks. To move the period to its correct place inside the quotation marks, use Search and Replace to change *xx"*. to *xx."* every time it appears.

Punctuation marks are road signs to help the reader: Slow down, detour, stop. Too much punctuation makes writing choppy, too little creates confusion. Its purpose is to clarify meaning, not erect roadblocks. Use it with that in mind.

APOSTROPHES

Apostrophes primarily show possession or a contraction. They are also used with certain plurals.

Use an apostrophe to show possession.

Add *'s* to singular words and to plural words not ending in *s*.
    the jury's verdict
    master's degree
    a friend of Joe's
    Miss Arkansas's victory
    Descartes's theorem
    Marx's philosophy

Malcolm Forbes, Jr.'s editorial
the twin's room (one person)
Charles's coat
Dylan Thomas's poems
the witness's testimony (one witness)
Jane Nelson's job

Today's rebel is tomorrow's tyrant.—Will and Ariel Durant

It is easier to love humanity as a whole than to love one's neighbor.—Eric Hoffer

Note that when you want the final *sis* or *siz* sound to be pronounced, you should add *'s* rather than just the apostrophe.

Add only the apostrophe to plural words that end in *s* or to singular words ending in *s* where you want to avoid adding a *sis* or *siz* sound.
Mr. and Mrs. Jones' suitcase
the judges' rulings
states' rights
the Joneses' suitcase
the puppies' food
the twins' room (two people)
the witnesses' testimony (more than one witness)
the Prince of Wales' appearance
the Nelsons' house

To avoid such common errors as "the Nelson's house," first make the word plural (Nelsons), then make it possessive (Nelsons').

Add the possessive *'s* to the last word of a phrase or compound, such as:

> my brother-in-law's Porsche
> the Surgeon General's warning
> the Senator from Maine's vote

However, making a phrase possessive can get out of hand. Rewrite to avoid such monstrosities as *the officer who resigned last week's signature ... (the signature of the officer who resigned last week ...)*.

When there is joint ownership of a single item, add *'s* to the last name only.

> Laura and Tom's car (one car)
> Tom and Jerry's feud

When the ownership is not joint, add *'s* to each name.

> his sister's and brother's birthdays (two birthdays)
> men's, women's, and children's departments

Apostrophes are often omitted in names of organizations, institutions or countries that end in *s*, where the words are more descriptive than possessive.

> Teachers College   Publishers Weekly   Consumers Union
> United Nations delegate   United States diplomat

Apostrophes are usually—but not always—used in organization names that do not end in *s*.

> Longshoremen's Union   McDonald's

but   Childrens Hospital *or* Children's Hospital

Find a reasonably reliable source of information about a given name (phonebook, letterhead) and use that form.

Use an apostrophe to show a contraction or omission.

won't (will not)	can't (cannot)
o'clock (of the clock)	haven't (have not)
ma'am (madam)	there's (there is)
Spirit of '76	coup d'état
it's (it is)	

As usual, there's a great woman behind every idiot.
—John Lennon

Be awful nice to 'em going up, because you're gonna meet 'em all comin' down. —Jimmy Durante

Note: *It's* is a contraction of *it is* or *it has*; *its* (without the apostrophe) is a possessive pronoun.

Contraction: *It's not the men in my life that counts—it's the life in my men.* —Mae West

Possession: *There is more to life than increasing its speed.* —Mohandas K. Gandhi

Use the apostrophe to show duration.

one minute's delay
two weeks' vacation
ten years' experience

Canada has a climate of nine months' winter and three months late in the fall.

Add an apostrophe to the word preceding a gerund.

in the event of Milford's resigning.
I object to the visitor's speaking French.
(Notice how the meaning would change in the last example if the *'s* were omitted.)

Use an apostrophe with certain plurals.

do's and don'ts	Ph.D.'s
2 by 4's	M.D.'s
p's and q's	M.P.'s

There are two *c's* in *accumulate*.

Don't use apostrophes in the following cases:

Change:	**to:**
keeping up with the Jones's	keeping up with the Joneses
"The Red Pony"'s ending	the ending of "The Red Pony"
Yankee's, go home	Yankees, go home
the three R's	the three Rs
the late 1960's	the late 1960s
the Roaring '20's	the Roaring '20s *or* Twenties
one's and two's	ones and twos
COD's	CODs

but when there are periods (C.O.D.'s) or you are showing possession rather than a plural (the SEC's recommendation), use the apostrophe.

Correct but awkward:	Rewrite:
my and my sister's room	This room is my sister's and mine.

COLONS

Colons introduce something that follows: definitions, explanations, summaries, lists, examples, and so on. The first word following the colon is capitalized if it begins a complete sentence. Colons also provide separation in certain situations.

Use a colon to introduce something.

To be positive: to be mistaken at the top of one's voice.
—Ambrose Bierce

Peter Drucker expresses one view: The computer is a moron.

There are two times in a man's life when he shouldn't speculate: when he can't afford it, and when he can.—Mark Twain

The difference between intelligence and education is this: Intelligence will make you a good living.—Charles F. Kettering

There are two ways of disliking poetry: one way is to dislike it, the other is to read Pope.—Oscar Wilde

Asked to distinguish between a misfortune and a calamity, Disraeli quipped:

> If Gladstone fell into the Thames, that would be a misfortune, and if anybody pulled him out that, I suppose, would be a calamity.

The results of the survey may be summarized in this way: in favor of rezoning, 59%; opposed, 41%.

Carney's Law: There's at least a 50-50 chance that someone will print the name Craney incorrectly.—Jim Canrey

Use a colon to separate certain words or numbers.

Better Letters: A Handbook of Business & Personal Correspondence

Congressional Directory, Washington: U.S. Government Printing Office

Computer Wimp (1983, Berkeley: Ten Speed Press)

12:30 p.m.   Matthew 6:3-7   *Nature* 3:127-9

Dear Mr. Abbott:

a ratio of 2:1   proportions of 5:3:1

Don't use colons in these cases:

• to introduce words that would fit smoothly into the sentence without a colon.

Wrong: Lewis Carroll defines arithmetic as: ambition, distraction, uglification, and derision.

Right: Lewis Carroll defines arithmetic as ambition, distraction ...

Wrong: The effects of the reorganization are: an increase in productivity and a reduction in absenteeism and personnel turnover.

Right: The effects of the reorganization are an increase ...

Wrong: The confiscated drugs included: marijuana, cocaine, and heroin.

Right: The confiscated drugs included marijuana, cocaine, and heroin.

• when the word "follows" or "following" does not *immediately* precede whatever is listed.

Wrong: A list of those attending follows. Notice that management and labor are equally represented:
          Marilyn Tompkins
          Clay Jensen
          Sylvia Warner ...

Right: A list of those attending follows. Notice that management and labor are equally represented.
          Marilyn Tompkins
          Clay Jensen
          Sylvia Warner ...

COMMAS

Commas prevent misreading. They clarify meaning and help the reader grasp the relation of parts of the sentence more quickly. However, unnecessary commas are a greater distraction than omitted ones, so add only those that promote ease of reading.

Use a comma in the following:

in compound sentences, to separate independent clauses

A doctor can bury his mistakes, but an architect can only advise his client to plant vines.—Frank Lloyd Wright

Opportunities are usually disguised as hard work, so most people don't recognize them.—Ann Landers

We can lick gravity, but sometimes the paperwork is overwhelming.
—Wernher von Braun

with nonrestrictive clauses

I would venture to guess that Anon., who wrote so many poems without signing them, was often a woman.—Virginia Woolf

following participial phrases

Thrusting my nose firmly between his teeth, I threw him heavily to the ground on top of me.—Mark Twain

to indicate a pause or break in continuity

No matter how thin you slice it, it's still baloney.—Alfred E. Smith

A bore is a man who, when you ask him how he is, tells you.
—Bert Taylor

when addressing someone directly

Depend upon it, sir, when a man knows he is to be hanged in a fortnight, it concentrates his mind wonderfully.
—Samuel Johnson

Lady Astor: *Winston, if you were my husband, I should flavor your coffee with poison.*
Churchill: *Madam, if I were your husband, I should drink it.*

with appositives

Hoffer, our resident Peasant Philosopher, is an example of articulate ignorance.—John Seelye

The first problem for all of us, men and women, is not to learn, but to unlearn.—Gloria Steinem

with coordinate adjectives

a tall, stately redwood

I found him a plausible, attractive rogue, all nervous energy and wit.
—Thomas Flanagan

with complementary or contrasting elements

Skepticism, like chastity, should not be relinquished too readily.
—George Santayana

Much outcry, little outcome.—Aesop

This novel is not to be tossed lightly aside, but to be hurled with great force.—Dorothy Parker

following introductory phrases

As a general rule, nobody has money who ought to have it.
—Benjamin Disraeli

In the main, opera in English is just about as sensible as baseball in Italian.—H.L. Mencken

in a series

Talk low, talk slow, and don't say too much.—John Wayne

The only things that evolve by themselves in an organization are disorder, friction, and malperformance.—Peter Drucker

Note: Some consider the final comma in a series to be optional. However, by always adding the final comma, you avoid potential confusion.

Unclear: Two developments will affect pregnancy, birth and infants.
Clear: Two developments will affect pregnancy, birth, and infants.

for clarity

Those who borrow, regret it.

Everybody is ignorant, only on different subjects. —Will Rogers

If she chooses, Adams can apply for an extension.

with identical words or unrelated numbers

Difficult though it may be, be open to change.

Total enrollment is 24, 15 of whom hold advanced degrees.

to show omission

You are apprehensive of monarchy; I, of aristocracy.
—John Adams

with quotations

Billy Rose said, "Never invest your money in anything that eats or needs repairing."

with a stated question or dictum

The first and great commandment is, Don't let them scare you.
—Elmer Davis

when the modifier follows the modified

The shareholders' meeting, tense and divisive, lasted four hours.

with titles

Oliver Wendell Holmes, Jr.
Laura M. Schmidt, Attorney at Law
Helen Cardwell, M.D.
Steven R. Klein, Management Consultant

following opening subordinate clauses

If you can count your money, you don't have a billion dollars.
—J. Paul Getty

When a man retires and time is no longer a matter of urgent importance, his colleagues generally present him with a watch.
—R.C. Sherriff

If this is the way Queen Victoria treats her convicts, she doesn't deserve to have any. —Oscar Wilde

with parenthetical expressions

It requires an unusual mind, according to Alfred North Whitehead, to analyze the obvious.

Prophecy, however honest, is generally a poor substitute for experience. —Justice Benjamin N. Cardozo

Don't use commas in the following cases:

- between short, closely related clauses:

  > *Some carve great careers while others simply chisel.*
  > —Laurence J. Peter

- between an independent and a dependent clause:

  > *Management by objectives works if you know the objectives.*
  > —Peter Drucker

  > *Don't talk unless you can improve the silence.* —Vermont proverb

  > *Facts do not cease to exist because they are ignored.*
  > —Aldous Huxley

- with restrictive clauses:

  > *Too bad that all the people who know how to run the country are busy driving taxicabs and cutting hair.* —George Burns

  > *An optimist is a driver who thinks that an empty space at the curb won't have a hydrant beside it.* —Changing Times

  - *following* the last item in a series:

    His reports occasionally lapse into disorganized, incoherent, jargon-filled writing. (*not* jargon-filled, writing)

- between adjectives where the first modifies both the second adjective and the noun:

  > traditional political institutions

  > a snowy Christmas eve

DASHES

Dashes can usually be replaced by other punctuation marks. In formal or business writing, you should probably limit their use to situations where a dramatic emphasis is justified. Dashes are an interruption, like waving your finger under the reader's nose. Whenever a colon, semicolon, or comma would serve just as well, use it.

Poor:　Our concern is—will you be able to pay on time?
Better:　Our concern is, will you be able to pay on time?

Reserve dashes for an occasional change of pace, as in the following cases:

to emphasize what follows

Familiarity breeds contempt—and children.—Mark Twain

When I was six I made my mother a little hat—out of her new blouse.—Lilly Daché

to indicate an abrupt change or an afterthought

The business of government is to keep the government out of business—that is, unless business needs government aid.—Will Rogers

The best way to keep children home is to make the home atmosphere pleasant—and let the air out of the tires.—Dorothy Parker

to summarize or explain

They say a reasonable number of fleas is good for a dog—keeps him from broodin' over bein' a dog.—E.N. Westcott

A pedestrian is a man who has two cars—one being driven by his wife, the other by one of his children.—Robert Benchley

Business has only two basic functions—marketing and innovation.—Peter Drucker

Dashes can be combined with exclamation marks, question marks, and quotation marks.

Her response was emphatic—"I will not sign."
His response surprised us—were you expecting it?

Do not combine dashes with commas, colons, semicolons, or parentheses.

Wrong:　The books—all 12 of them, were overdue.
Right:　The books—all 12 of them—were overdue.

Those who have desktop publishing capabilities should know when to use the em dash (—) and the en dash (–). The above examples call for an em dash. The en dash is primarily used to indicated inclusiveness.

1988–89   pp. 35–47   New York–Boston train

A 2-em dash indicates omitted letters (Ms. T——, D——d right!). A 3-em dash replaces entire words, as in a bibliography where it is used instead of repeating an author's name.

On a standard typewriter keyboard, an em dash is indicated by two hyphens, an en dash by one hyphen.

ELLIPSES

Use an ellipsis (three periods) when showing an omission within quoted material.

A great many people have ... asked how I manage to get so much work done and still keep looking so dissipated.
—Robert Benchley

If the ellipsis *follows* a sentence, end the sentence with its appropriate punctuation mark (e.g., period, question mark) before adding the ellipsis.

The only way to get rid of temptation is to yield to it. ... I can resist everything but temptation.—Oscar Wilde

If the ellipsis *precedes* the period ending a sentence, use four periods.

An important scientific innovation rarely makes its way by gradually winning over and converting its opponents.... What does happen is that its opponents gradually die out....
—Max Planck

HYPHENS

Hyphens divide words at the end of the line (see Word Division, p. 158) and join certain words to form compounds (break-in, old-fashioned music). The rules for hyphenating words are lengthy and complex; they are also riddled with exceptions. Many words that used to be hyphenated are now written as one word. Examples are probably the most useful learning tool, so the following paragraphs are short on rules and long on examples.

If you take hyphens seriously, you will surely go mad.
—John Benbow

Hyphenate a few prefixes.

anti-hero   ex-husband   post-mortem

Today, most prefixes are not hyphenated.

preempt	microorganism	reenter
macroeconomics	interrelated	semiconductor
microcomputer	infrastructure	bipartisan

However, retain the hyphen in the following cases.

• when confusion or an awkward pronunciation results from the one-word form:

co-owner   re-read   co-opt   un-ionized   co-worker

• when the root word is capitalized:

anti-American pro-Israeli pre-Columbian post-World War I

• when the second part of a hyphenated term consists of two or more words:

non-tumor-bearing tissue   pre-gold-strike era
ultra-high-speed device   three-ring-circus atmosphere

• when certain double or triple letters would occur:

anti-intellectual   shell-like   semi-independent   non-native

Hyphenate fractions and compound numbers.

one-third   forty-seven

Hyphenate to show a range of numbers:

1894-1898   pp. 89-92

Notice the following usage:

Wrong: Candidates must be from 35-50 years old.
Right: Candidates must be from 35 to 50 years old.   *or*
Candidates must be 35-50 years old.

Hyphenate to combine a numeral and noun or adjective (a unit modifier).

1/2-acre lot   5-ml beaker   10-kilometer run
75-page report   50-odd members

Hyphenate certain compounds.

When you are deciding whether to hyphenate a compound word, be guided by the goal of making your writing easy to understand. *An old film buff* describes an elderly person who enjoys movies. *An old-film buff* is someone who enjoys old films. Your meaning determines whether you use the hyphen.

Hyphenate to prevent misreading in such cases as the following.

Adjectives

good-natured response
fast-talking salesman
stiff-necked attitude
panic-stricken audience
economy-sized package
long-term effects
double-barreled proposition
sway-backed horse

thought-provoking statement
ill-fed people
in-house memo
dog-eared book
double-decker bus
grain-fed beef
time-honored custom
three-ring circus

The best mind-altering drug is truth. —Lily Tomlin

That enfabled rock, that ship of life, that swarming million-footed, tower-masted, and sky-soaring citadel that bears the name of the Island of Manhattan. —Thomas Wolfe

Brevity is only skin deep, and the world is full of thin-skinned people. —Richard Armour

Nouns

poet-statesman   well-wisher   write-off   know-how
go-between   ne'er-do-well   break-in   page-turner

There are no whole truths; all truths are half-truths.
—Alfred North Whitehead

Improvised Compounds

touch-me-not   stick-to-itiveness   Johnny-come-lately
topsy-turvy   dog-eat-dog   do-it-yourself

Nowadays people are divided into three classes—the Haves, the Have-nots, and the Have-Not-Paid-for-What-They-Haves.
—Earl Wilson

Omit hyphens in established compounds when they are not needed to clarify meaning.

city hall news	White House staff
real estate office	high school dropout

See p. 154 for a more complete discussion of the formation of compound words.

Don't use hyphens in the following cases:

coordinate	postdoctoral
antiwar	bilateral
catlike	statewide
publicly held stock	transcontinental
overanxious	midtown
metalanguage	underfunded

Also, never hyphenate a word ending in *-ly.*

Wrong: widely-known author, commonly-held assumption
Right: widely known author, commonly held assumption

QUOTATION MARKS

Quotation marks set off spoken words; they are also used to differentiate words or phrases from the surrounding text. Single quotation marks enclose quoted material within a quotation.

Place the period and comma *inside* the closing quotation mark. (British usage calls for the period outside the closing quotation.) Place all other punctuation *outside* the closing quotation mark, unless it is part of what is quoted. Capitalize the first word in a quotation, unless an ellipsis (...) indicates that the quotation begins in mid-sentence. Each of the following examples illustrates an aspect of the rules associated with quotation marks.

Twenty million young women rose to their feet with the cry "We will not be dictated to," and promptly became stenographers.
—G.K. Chesterton

Today's "fact" becomes tomorrow's "misinformation."
—Alvin Toffler

When the government talks about "raising capital" it means printing it.—Peter Drucker

Diplomacy is the art of saying "Nice doggie!" till you can find a rock.—Wynn Catlin

"Out of sight, out of mind," when translated into Russian by computer, then back again into English, became "invisible maniac."

Dr. Karl Menninger said, "Generous people are rarely mentally ill people."

He shouted, "Man overboard!"

The bride and groom said their "I Do's."

Do you know the words to "The Star-Spangled Banner"?

Thoreau asked the question, "What is the use of a house if you haven't got a tolerable planet to put it on?"

The package was marked "Refused—Return to Sender."

His "education" consisted of a hard right to the jaw.

"Money won't buy happiness," according to Bill Vaughan, "but it will pay the salaries of a large research staff to study the problem."

I prefer the word "homemaker" because "housewife" implies that there may be a wife someplace else.—Bella Abzug

A quote within a quote is indicated by single quotation marks.

> Richard Armour quipped, "That money talks I'll not deny. I heard it once: It said, 'Goodbye.'"

> Ed Howe is reported to have said, "When I say 'Everybody says so,' I mean *I* say so."

> Kin Hubbard asked, "Why don't th' feller who says, 'I'm not a speechmaker,' let it go at that instead of giving a demonstration?"

You may alter capitalization to make a quotation fit into a sentence. For example:

> E. F. Schumacher urged us to understand that "small is beautiful."
> (not ... "Small is Beautiful.")

In legal or scholarly writing, use brackets to show where you have added a word or capital letter.

> *The history of our time is a history of phrases, which rise to great power and then suddenly pass away: "the merchants of death," ... "America first," "cash and carry," ... "bring the boys home," ... [F]ew men have had either the courage or the resources to stand up to these shibboleths.* —Russell Davenport

With quotations of more than one paragraph, you have two choices.

(1) Place quotation marks at the *beginning* of each paragraph but at the *end* of only the *final* paragraph.

(2) Indent the quotation as a block and use no quotation marks.

Don't use quotation marks in the following cases:

Charles Dudley Warner observed that the thing generally raised on city land is taxes.

The question remained, Who was responsible?

Samuel Clemens, better known as Mark Twain, . . .

The so-called gender gap has taken on political overtones. (*not* the so-called "gender gap")

Learning when to say no is an important lesson in business.

Be sure to place the quotation mark where the quotation actually begins.

Wrong: This is helpful to the female employee who may not understand "that all salesmen must turn in expense vouchers" includes her.

Right: This is helpful to the female employee who may not understand that "all salesmen must turn in expense vouchers" includes her.

SEMICOLONS

The semicolon produces a more emphatic break than a comma. Use semicolons when you want a stronger pause than a comma but less separation than two sentences.

Use a semicolon between independent clauses.

Beware of little expenses; a small leak will sink a great ship.
—Benjamin Franklin

The brain is a wonderful organ; it starts working the moment you get up in the morning and doesn't stop until you get to the office.
—Robert Frost

Wit has truth in it; wisecracking is simply calisthenics with words.
—Dorothy Parker

Hanging is too good for a man who makes puns; he should be drawn and quoted.—Fred Allen

One friend in a lifetime is much; two are many; three are hardly possible.—Henry Adams

Time is change; we measure its passage by how much things alter.
—Nadine Gordimer

A man with one watch knows what time it is; a man with two watches is never quite sure.—Lee Segall

Use a semicolon between items in a series that contains commas.

If a man runs after money, he's money-mad; if he keeps it, he's a capitalist; it he spends it, he's a playboy; if he doesn't get it, he's a ne'er-do-well; if he doesn't try to get it, he lacks ambition. If he gets it without working for it, he's a parasite; and if he accumulates it after a lifetime of hard work, people call him a fool who never got anything out of life.—Vic Oliver.

Don't use a semicolon between an independent clause and a dependent (or subordinate) clause.

Wrong: The project will not be funded; even though it is worthwhile.
Right: The project will not be funded even though it is worthwhile.

Chapter 7

Second-Level Editing:

Grammar

Chapter 7.
SECOND-LEVEL EDITING: GRAMMAR

Good grammar is transparent. It doesn't draw attention to itself, prompting readers to think "This sure is good grammar." The readers just know they understand what is written and that it flows smoothly. Grammatical errors, on the other hand, probably don't trumpet their presence with names such as Misplaced Modifiers or Unparallel Construction. But readers know they have been confused, jarred, or frustrated. They resent wasting time trying to fathom the intended meaning.

Most people use grammatical rules without being aware of them. Somehow the rules have been assimilated unconsciously. But occasionally a question comes up: Should a verb be singular or plural? Is *I, me,* or *myself* correct? Which is better—*if it was* or *if it were*? Knowing the rules (or where to find them) answers such questions.

This section covers the six areas where most grammatical questions arise. Use these guidelines to sharpen your awareness of potential problems. The examples and rules will help you detect and correct errors in agreement, misplaced modifiers, and so on.

AGREEMENT

Every part of a sentence should agree with every related part. This means that every subject and verb should agree in number (i.e., be either singular or plural) and that every pronoun and antecedent should agree.

Subject and verb should agree in number.

A singular subject requires a singular verb:

> *The wastepaper basket is a writer's best friend.*
> —Isaac Bashevis Singer
> (singular subject, *basket*; singular verb, *is*)

A plural subject requires a plural verb:

> *We are confronted with insurmountable opportunities.*
> —Pogo (Walt Kelly)
>   (plural subject, *we*; plural verb, *are confronted*)

The verb must also agree with the subject when the subject follows the verb:

> What are the answers?
> There is one doctor.
> Answering questions from the press were three candidates.
>
> *Behind the phoney tinsel of Hollywood lies the real tinsel.*
> —Oscar Levant

A compound subject joined by *and* requires a plural verb:

> *The rich man and his daughter are soon parted.* —Kin Hubbard
>
> Completing the form and mailing it promptly are important.
>
> *Only presidents, editors, and people with tapeworms have the right to use the editorial "we."* —Mark Twain

A compound subject joined by *or* or *nor* takes a singular verb:

> A passport or tourist card is necessary.

Some compound subjects are treated as a unit and thus take a singular verb:

> Meat and potatoes is standard fare.
> Heidrick & Struggles is a national firm.

A compound subject **preceded** by the word *each* or *every* is singular:

> Each question and answer was carefully considered.
> Every representative and senator is on our mailing list.

As well as preceding a word or phrase does not affect the number of the verb.

> The owner, as well as his employees, is implicated.

In *either/or* and *neither/nor* constructions, the verb agrees with the nearest subject:

> Either the equipment or the samples were contaminated.
> Neither envelopes nor letterhead was delivered.

The number of the verb is not affected by intervening phrases:

> Working conditions, a subject of frequent debate, are ...
> The results, including an unexpected side effect, are ...
> The briefcase with the missing reports is ...
> The verb in the main clause of each of these examples is ...
> The verbs in each sentence are ...
> One in every ten components is ...

Treat the following indefinite pronouns as singular: each, each one, every, everyone, everybody, either, neither, nobody, no one, any, anyone, anybody, somebody, someone.

> *In the United States there is more space where nobody is than where anybody is.* —Gertrude Stein

> Each is expensive.

However, when *each* **follows** a plural subject, the verb is plural.

> The teachers each have different ideas for solving the problem.

Treat the following indefinite pronouns either as singular or plural, depending on the context or meaning: none, some, more, all, most, half.

> *All's fair in love and war.* —Francis Edward Smedley

> *All want to be learned, but none is willing to pay the price.*
> —Juvenal

> *More is experienced in one day in the life of a learned man than in the whole lifetime of an ignorant man.* —Seneca

> More are experienced programmers than in previous years.

The word *none* is singular when it means *no one* or *not one*, plural when it means *not any* or *no amount*.

> None of the missing documents was found.

> Three manuscripts were submitted, but none are ready for publication.

The word *number* is singular when preceded by *the*, plural when preceded by *a*.

> The number of mistakes was small.
> A number of mistakes were made.

Treat the following indefinite pronouns as plural: few, both, many, others, several.

> A few are ready; the others are ill-prepared.

Collective nouns (such as family, group, committee, couple, team, personnel, staff, majority) are singular unless they refer to individuals within the group.

> The personnel were screened for verbal and mathematical aptitudes. (Individuals within the group were screened.)
> The team was late. (The group is treated as a unit.)

> The contents of the test tube was withdrawn. (as a whole)
> The contents of the package were examined. (as individual elements)

> The staff supports the move.
> The majority are unwilling to contribute.

A subject that expresses a sum, rate, measurement, or quantity as a unit takes a singular verb even when the subject is plural.

> Three centimeters is more than one inch.
> Five dollars is a reasonable price.

Some words ending in *s* appear to be plural but are actually a singular concept: news, physics, economics, series.

> The news is good.
> The series of tests was completed.

Some words are either singular or plural, depending on their use: statistics, politics.

> *Facts are stubborn, but statistics are more pliable.*
> —Laurence J. Peter

> *Politics is the science of who gets what, when, and why.*
> —Sidney Hillman

> My politics are my own affair.

Some have no singular form and require a plural verb.

> scissors, pliers, forceps, trousers, slacks

Handle relative pronouns as follows: *who, which,* and *that* take singular verbs when referring to singular words, plural verbs when referring to plural words.

Singular: *Anyone who hates children and dogs can't be all bad.*
   —W.C. Fields

Plural: *People who bite the hand that feeds them usually lick the boot that kicks them.* —Eric Hoffer

What takes a singular verb, unless it has a plural antecedent:

> *What kills a skunk is the publicity it gives itself.*
> —Abraham Lincoln

Agreement should be between verb and subject, not between verb and complement:

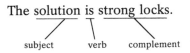

The solution is strong locks.

subject   verb   complement

When the subject is a phrase or clause, use a singular verb.

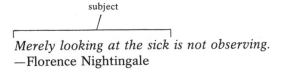

subject

Merely looking at the sick is not observing.
—Florence Nightingale

Pronoun and antecedent should agree in number.

All *employees* must provide *their* own tools.

He is a self-made man and worships his creator.
—William Cowper

Whatever women do they must do twice as well as men to be thought half as good. Luckily, this is not difficult.
—Charlotte Whitton

When the jury returns to give its verdict ...

Neither Karen nor Linda would break her silence.
    (compounds joined by *or* or *nor* are singular)

Men are never so tired and harassed as when they have to deal with a woman who wants a raise.—Michael Korda

Latin Words

Certain commonly used Latin words are frequently the source of errors of agreement (*phenomena, criteria*). The table on p. 76 shows which words have retained their Latin plurals and which have been Anglicized.

PRONOUNS

Use pronouns in their correct case.

nominative	*possessive*	*objective*
I	my	me
you	your	you
he	his	him
she	her	her
it	its	it
we	our	us
they	their	them
who	whose	whom

Use the nominative case when the pronoun is the subject:

> *People who say they sleep like a baby usually don't have one.*
> —Leo J. Burke
>> (*who* is the subject of the verb *say, they* is the subject of the verb *sleep*)

Wilson and I will attend.

Use the possessive case when you want to show ownership.

> *I should have the courage of my lack of conviction.*
> —Tom Stoppard

Wilson and Gaines missed their flight.

Use the objective case when the pronoun is the object of a verb or preposition.

> *Marriage is the alliance of two people, one of whom never remembers birthdays and the other never forgets them.*
> —Ogden Nash
>> (*whom* is the object of the preposition *of, them* is the object of the verb *forgets*)

Submit the report to Wilson and me.

Once you've determined the correct case, you know which pronoun to use (for example, *I* or *me*, *who* or *whom*).

> The seats were given to the oldest passengers, Wilson and (*I* or *me*).

The choice becomes easy if you mentally eliminate everything between the verb or preposition and the pronoun whose case you're trying to determine. Try it in the above example.

The seats were given to ... (*I* or *me*).

The correct pronoun is *me*.

Wrong: The contest has narrowed down to you and I.
Right: The content has narrowed down to you and me.

Wrong: Send the questionnaire to whomever wants a copy.
Right: Send the questionnaire to whoever wants a copy.
      (*whoever* is the subject of the verb *wants* in the dependent clause "whoever wants a copy")

Wrong: The woman who we hired has an MBA.
Right: The woman whom we hired has an MBA.
      (*whom* is the object of the verb *hired*)

When in doubt about *who* or *whom*, substitute a personal pronoun for the word. If a nominative pronoun feels right (*I, we, she*), use *who*, which is the nominative form of the word. If an objective pronoun fits (*me, us, her*), use *whom*.

The first person *who* answers all questions correctly ...
      (*he* answers all questions ...)

Levy is the man *whom* I invited for dinner.
      (I invited *him*).

Following *than* or *as*, mentally insert the missing verbs to determine the correct case of the pronoun.

I am as hard-working as *he* [is].

The supervisor corrects Klein more often than [she corrects] *me*.

The supervisor corrects Klein more often than *I* [do].

Avoid unnecessary reflexive or intensive pronouns (pronouns ending in *-self* or *-selves*).

Wrong: The summons was received by my partner and myself.
Right: The summons was received by my partner and me.

Wrong: My partner and myself received ...
Right: My partner and I received ...

This error is especially common with the first person, perhaps because *myself* or *ourselves* seems less presumptuous than *I* or *we*. A reflexive pronoun is correctly used when it refers back to the subject:

> He shot himself.

An intensive pronoun is used for emphasis.

> I will present the award myself.

Make pronouns refer clearly to their antecedents.

Pronouns are stand-ins for another word or group of words (their antecedents). Therefore, what the pronoun is standing in for or referring to must always be clear to the reader.

A series of ambiguous pronouns creates confusion.

Unclear: She told her that her secretary had typed her resignation.
(Whose secretary? Whose resignation?)

A single ambiguous pronoun can be just as baffling.

Clear: Company A is losing sales to Company B and its competitors.
(Whose competitors, A's or B's?)

Sometimes the antecedent is missing entirely.

Unclear: When you calculate the number of managers and subordinates, it is eye-opening.
(What does *it* refer to? Probably the ratio of managers to subordinates, which appears in the sentence only indirectly. Rewrite.)

Clear: When you calculate the number of managers and subordinates, the ratio is eye-opening.

ADJECTIVES AND ADVERBS

Use adjectives to modify nouns or pronouns; use adverbs to modify verbs, adjectives, or other adverbs.

The following examples illustrate correct usage.

> She gave a *quick* answer. (adj., modifies the noun *answer*; it describes what kind of answer)

She answered *quickly.* (adv., modifies the verb *answer*; it tells how she answered)

a *public* company (adj., modifies the noun *company*)
a *publicly* held company (adv., modifies the adjective *held*)

The reporter was *uncertain.* (adj., modifies *reporter*)
The reporter answered *uncertainly* (adv., modifies *answered*)

I feel *bad* about the mixup. (adj., modifies the pronoun *I*)
I feel *badly* treated. (adv., modifies the verb *treated*)

Again, words that end in *-ly* should not be hyphenated.

Put modifiers where they will produce the desired meaning.

Wrong: People who eat wild mushrooms often die.
Right: Often, people who eat wild mushrooms die.

Wrong: Children are sometimes placed in Juvenile Hall because there are inadequate foster homes to meet their needs.

The homes may indeed be inadequate, but the following sentence probably has the intended meaning.

Right: Children are sometimes placed in Juvenile Hall because of an inadequate supply of foster homes.

Have you chosen the best modifier for the job?

Wrong: The chemical dissolves readily and only a small dose can be fatal.

A large dose cannot? Replacing "only" with "even" makes a sensible sentence.

Compare the following sentences in which the word *only* appears in different places. Whichever one accurately reflects the circumstances is the correct version.

The invitation said that **only** the press could attend the dress rehearsal.

The invitation said that the press could **only** attend the dress rehearsal.

The invitation said that the press could attend **only** the dress rehearsal.

In general, place modifiers close to the words they modify.

Misplaced modifiers often produce ambiguous or unintentionally humorous results.

> You can order a rental car that will be delivered to your home by telephone.

> The critics recommended "Why John and Joan Can't Read," a documentary that reveals the shocking state of adult illiteracy on public television.

> The patient has had chest pain when she lies on her left side for over a year.

> The chimpanzees were observed using binoculars.

> Staff members should submit a completed travel voucher with the required receipts attached to their department heads.

Dangling modifiers are another common error of placement. A dangler usually begins the sentence; what it modifies has been omitted.

> Checking the records, the error was found.

Since "the error" cannot have been "checking the records," the opening phrase is left dangling. Add the correct subject to the main clause to remedy the situation.

> Checking the records, she found the error.

Here are some other dangling modifiers. Watch for such illogical constructions and rewrite to include the correct subject.

Dangler: Red-eyed from fatigue, Jim's voice cracked with emotion.
Correct: Red-eyed from fatigue, Jim spoke in a voice that cracked with emotion.

Dangler: Having read the instructions carefully, my bicycle was easily assembled.

Correct: Having read the instructions carefully, I was able to assemble my bicycle easily.

Dangler: On arriving at the third floor, her apartment is the first door on the left.

Correct: On arriving at the third floor, you will find her apartment at the first door on the left.

VERBS

Use the correct tense.

The correct tense comes naturally to most native-born writers. A tense that sounds right probably is right.

Present: I walk

Past: I walked

Future: I will walk

Present Perfect: I have walked (an action that began in the past and continues to or is completed in the present)

Past Perfect: I had walked (an action that began and was completed in the past)

Future Perfect: I will have walked (an action that will begin in the future and be completed by a specific time)

Yesterday I was a dog. Today I'm a dog. Tomorrow I'll probably still be a dog. Sigh. There's so little hope for advancement. —Snoopy (Charles Schulz)

Where problems usually arise is in maintaining logical consistency. If you have chosen the present tense to describe a marketing study ("Our survey **shows** ... "), use the present tense throughout ("that both men and women **prefer** ... "). Especially when editing a long document, read it once just to check whether you have used tenses logically and consistently.

Here are two examples of areas where decisions about tense are needed.

He wondered whether the system (was) (is) fair.

The manager explained how the system (works) (worked).

In these examples, the past tense of the first verbs (*wondered, explained*) dictates that verbs in the dependent clauses that follow also be in the past tense. Thus, *was* and *worked* are the correct choices.

An exception is a statement of "universal truth" which calls for the present tense even when the main verb is in the past tense.

> Newton discovered (past tense) that apples fall (present tense).

> Benjamin Franklin knew that creditors have better memories than debtors.

The first verb in each of the following examples is in the perfect tense. What is the correct tense for subsequent verbs? (The choices are shown in parentheses.)

> They would have liked (to be) (to have been) the winners.

> Simpson has enjoyed (being) (having been) governor.

> It would have been easy for the department (to change) (to have changed) the procedure.

Piling up perfect tenses produces an almost tongue-twisting effect (would have liked to have been, has enjoyed having been, would have been easy ... to have changed). Logic also suggests that subsequent verbs be in the present tense, unless their action precedes the main verb. Correct choices in these examples are:

> They would have liked to be the winners.

> Simpson has enjoyed being governor.

> It would have been easy for the department to change the procedure.

Use the correct mood.

Most of our sentences are in the **indicative** mood.

> *Invention is the mother of necessity.*—Thorstein Veblen

The **interrogative** mood asks a question.

> *I am responsible for my actions, but who is responsible for General Motors?*—Ralph Nader

Commands and most instructions are in the **imperative** mood.

Press the red lever.

Fly me.—Freddie Laker

Be obscure clearly.—E. B. White

The **subjunctive** mood is used in only a few circumstances in today's writing. The subjunctive forms you will probably need to know for those occasions are as follows:

Indicative	*Subjunctive*
was	were
is	be
thinks (talks, drives, etc.)	think (talk, drive, etc.)

The following situations still call for the subjunctive mood:

• An improbable condition or one that is contrary to fact.
    If I *were* younger, I would challenge you to a match.

• An indirect command.
    She specified that the money *be* donated to charity.
    His friend insisted that he *drive* the car.

• Motions and resolutions.
    I move that the motion *be* adopted.

    Resolved, that the question *be submitted* to the full membership.

Shall or Will? The traditional distinction between *shall* and *will* has all but disappeared. *Will* has generally replaced *shall* in all future tenses. *Shall* still appears in some government and legal writing, where it probably results from the mistaken belief that *shall* sounds more authoritative.

Stilted: The contractor shall provide all the necessary materials.

Natural: The contractor will provide all the necessary materials.

Shall is appropriately used as a polite question, where it substitutes for *let's*.

    Shall we leave now?

PARALLEL STRUCTURE

Make related parts of a sentence or heading parallel in form.

This helps readers grasp the connection between the parallel elements and thus helps them understand your meaning. Aesthetics and dramatic effect are also enhanced. "Give me liberty or kill me" wouldn't have gone far in stirring patriotism.

Unparallel construction has been described as 1, 2, 3, A. You set up expectations by establishing a pattern and then you abandon it. In the process, you may create confusion.

To create parallel structure, make an infinitive parallel with an infinitive, an adjective with an adjective, and so on. In the following example, four active verbs are followed, unnecessarily, by a passive verb.

Unparallel: At the meeting we will (1) review the proposed ordinance, (2) discuss its legal implications, (3) listen to citizen comments, (4) take a vote, and (5) the meeting will then be adjourned.

Parallel: At the meeting we will (1) review the proposed ordinance, (2) discuss its legal implications, (3) listen to citizen comments, (4) take a vote, and (5) adjourn.

Unparallel: The new receptionist is efficient, unflappable, and has a friendly manner.

Parallel: The new receptionist is efficient, unflappable, and friendly.

Unparallel: A moment not only of suspense but excitement ...

Parallel: A moment not only of suspense but of excitement ...

Unparallel: The description was both accurate and it was easy to read.

Parallel: The description was both accurate and readable.

Unparallel: Either I will be late or do a poor job.

If *either* is followed by a complete clause (I will be late), *or* must also be followed by a complete clause (I will do a poor job). An alternative is to move *either*.

Parallel: I will either be late or do a poor job.

Parallel: *Men should be either caressed or exterminated.*
—Machiavelli

SENTENCE FAULTS

Avoid run-ons.

Run-ons are two independent clauses joined only by a comma (called a *comma splice*) or by no punctuation (called a *fused sentence*). Rewrite run-ons as separate sentences or join them with a semicolon. A semicolon provides a stronger pause then a comma, a weaker pause than a period.

Run-ons with the word "however" are especially common.

Run-on: We had planned to move into the new building in May, however, construction delays forced us to change our plans.

Correct: We had planned to move into the new building in May. However, construction delays ...

We had planned to move into the new building in May; however, construction delays ...

Use fragments with care.

A *fragment* is a partial sentence. In his *Dictionary of Modern English Usage*, Fowler calls fragments "verbless sentences" that enliven writing by making it more like spoken language. Fragments are appropriate in dialogue or in a question-and-answer format.

Will they win? Not if we can help it.

They can be used sparingly for emphasis or to achieve a particular effect.

Our guarantee is good for one year. Without exception.

Avoid fragments in formal writing where their informality would be out of place. If you have trouble detecting fragments, study the following examples.

Fragment: Knowing that the meeting would be disrupted if she arrived late.

Complete: Knowing that the meeting would be disrupted if she arrived late, she was careful to be on time.

Fragment: Long but incomplete thoughts that masquerade, right up to the end, as complete thoughts.

Complete: Watch out for long but incomplete thoughts that masquerade, right up to the end, as complete thoughts.

Fragment: Work being a way to fill one's days and one's checking account.

Complete: Work is a way to fill one's days and one's checking account.

Reading good writing is an excellent way to absorb the rules discussed in this chapter. In the press of everyday affairs, we often read very little. Take time now and then to read some of the best classical and modern writers. It will give you enjoyment, insight, and appreciation of how to use words effectively.

From *Writing that Works*, by Kenneth Roman and Joel Raphaelson:

If you want to write better, read E.B. White. Read Hemingway. Read *The New Yorker*. Read *The Economist*. Read William James and Mark Twain and H.L. Mencken, Rebecca West and Barbara Tuchman and Art Buchwald.

You'll get the shapes and rhythms of good writing into your head. Reading good writing will help you more than reading *about* good writing—and it is a lot more fun.

Chapter 8

Second-Level Editing:

Mechanical Style

Chapter 8.
SECOND-LEVEL EDITING: MECHANICAL STYLE

When you edit for mechanics, you check such matters as spelling, capitalization, abbreviations, and word division. You also review numbers (should they be words or figures?) and document appearance and integrity (such as missing tables or gaps in page numbers). These mechanical elements of style distinguish a polished document from a flawed one.

A style sheet will help you keep track of the choices you have made: capitalization (Co-Prosperity Spheres), hyphenation (non-aligned nations), number treatment (three million or 3 million), spellings (catalog or catalogue), and the like. Chapter 2, Some Useful Tools, describes how to create a style sheet.

Use the rules and tables presented in this section to put the finishing touches on your writing; use a style sheet to make sure you have been consistent.

ABBREVIATIONS

Abbreviations are seldom appropriate in the text of formal business writing or general writing such as fiction, history, or news. They create an aura of sloppiness or suggest that you were too hurried to complete the words. But some words are always abbreviated (for example, *Mr.*) and certain abbreviations are acceptable if space is tight or if they avoid cumbersome repetition.

Footnotes, tables, lists, and bibliographies are prime candidates for abbreviations. Technical writing also makes heavy use of them. (Technical writers should refer to a style guide for their particular discipline for the final word on abbreviations.) The following paragraphs present rules for abbreviation in business writing and in writing for publication.

In general, give the full name or term the first time it appears, followed by the abbreviated version in parentheses. Then use only the abbreviation throughout the remainder of the document.

The trend is away from the use of periods, especially with units of measurement (lb, km) and with abbreviations consisting entirely of capital letters (IRS, FDR). However, periods can be used if needed to prevent confusion when the abbreviated form spells a word (in., no.). Do not use periods with acronyms (OPEC, COBOL, NATO) or with shortened forms of words (typo, stereo, the Fed, co-op, caps).

To make an abbreviation or acronym plural, add a lowercase s:

> MVPs   IQs

If the abbreviation has periods, add 's:

> Ph.D.'s   D.S.O.'s

Do not begin a sentence with a symbol or abbreviation other than a social title (Ms., Dr., Mrs.).

Wrong: No. 5 shaft was the scene of the cave-in.
Right: Number 5 shaft was the scene of the cave-in. *or*
        The cave-in occurred in the No. 5 shaft.

Right: Dr. Singh will be retiring in May.

Names and Titles

> Ms.   Mrs.   Mr.   Messrs.   Mmes.   Jr.   Sr.   Esq.
> M.D.   Ph.D.   M.A.   J.D.   M.P.   D.V.M.   LL.B.

Wrong: Hon. Hoskins, Rev. Kennedy, Gen. Grant, Sen. Thurston, D.A. Marilyn West

Right: the Honorable Doris L. Hoskins, Hon. Doris L. Hoskins; the Reverend James F. Kennedy, Rev. James F. Kennedy; General Grant, Gen. Ulysses S. Grant; Senator Thurston, Senator Maxwell Thurston; District Attorney Marilyn West

Note: Abbreviations are acceptable in tables, captions, etc., (e.g., Dist. Atty. Marilyn West, Sen. Maxwell Thurston).

Wrong:	**Right:**
Dr. Andrew P. Andrews, M.D.	Andrew P. Andrews, M.D.
Ms. Eileen M. O'Brien, Esq.	Eileen M. O'Brien, Esq.
Professor Leslie Monson, Ph.D.	Leslie Monson, Ph.D.

Wrong: Chas. Conklin, Wm. Deane
   J.F.K., F.D.R.

Right: Charles Conklin, William Deane
   JFK, FDR

Agencies and Organizations

AAAS   CBS   FDA   ILGWU   IOOF   CAB
AFL-CIO   NFL   OAS   NOW   SBA   SAE

Write out company names without abbreviations in straight text (Union Oil Company, Serendipity Associates, Southern Pacific Railway), unless the company is known primarily by its abbreviated form (IBM, RCA, NCR, TRW).

The words *Inc.* and *Ltd.* are usually dropped. Use the firm's letterhead as a guide to the preferred abbreviated form for such terms as Brothers (Bros.), Company (Co.), and (&), Corporation (Corp.), and Incorporated (Inc.).

If space is limited, abbreviate the following in addresses:

   Division (Div.)   Department (Dept.)
   Headquarters (Hdqrs. or HQ)   Agency (Agcy.)
   Subsidiary (Subs.)   Institute (Inst.)

Geographical Terms

N E S W   NE SE SW NW   ENE SSW NNE
E by SE   N by NW

St. Louis   St. Paul   *but*
Fort Worth   Port Arthur   Mount Vernon

USSR, UK, UAR   *or*   U.S.S.R., U.K., U.A.R.
U.S. Department of Agriculture   U.S.S. Enterprise
U.S. Circuit Court

United States is abbreviated when it is an adjective but is otherwise written out.

   He was glad to return to the United States.
   They felt that U.S. foreign policy was misguided.

State abbreviations consist of two capital letters with no period (AL, CO, OH).

Dates and Times

Jan., Feb., Mar., Apr., May, June, July, Aug., Sept., Oct., Nov., Dec.
or   Ja F Mr Ap My Je Jl Au S O N D

Mon., Tues., Wed., Thurs., Fri., Sat., Sun.

sec, second(s)   min, minute(s)   hr, h, hour(s)
da, d, day(s)   wk, week(s)   mo, month(s)   yr, year(s)

A.M. (*ante meridiem*)   P.M. (*post meridiem*)
M. (noon, *meridies*)   12 P.M. (midnight)

Parts of Books or Documents

References to parts of books or documents should be abbreviated
only when they appear in parentheses: (Chap. 4) or (Par. 9a).

Constitutions and Bylaws

Section and *Article* are spelled out the first time and abbreviated in
subsequent uses.

SECTION 1, ARTICLE 1   SEC. 2, ART. 2

Commercial Abbreviations

@	at	ea.	each
acct.	account	FOB	free on board
bal.	balance	mdse.	merchandise
bbl.	barrel	mfg.	manufacturing
bdl.	bundle	mfr.	manufacturer
COD	cash on delivery	OEM	original equipment
cr.	credit, creditor		manufacturer
cwt.	hundredweight	pd.	paid
doz.	dozen	std.	standard
dr.	debit, debtor		

Measurement

ac or AC	alternating current, air conditioning	lb	pound
A or amp	ampere	MHz	megahertz
Btu	British thermal unit	Mev	million electron volts
C	Celsius	mi	mile
cal	calorie	ml	milliliter
Cal	Kilocalorie	mo	month
cc	cubic centimeter	mm	millimeter
cm	centimeter	mpg	miles per gallon
cu	cubic	mph	miles per hour
db	decibel	oz	ounce
dc or DC	direct current	ppm	parts per million
doz	dozen	ppb	parts per billion
F	Fahrenheit	psi	pounds per square inch
FM	frequency modulation	qt	quart
ft	foot	r or R	roentgen
g	gram, gravity	rpm	revolutions per minute
gal	gallon	SD	standard deviation
hp	horsepower	s or sec	second
hr	hour	sq	square
hz	hertz	STP	standard temperature & pressure
in	inch	UHF	ultra high frequency
IQ	intelligence quotient	v	volt
IU	international unit	VHF	very high frequency
K	carat	w	watt
kHz	kilohertz	wk	week
kg	kilogram	yd	yard
km	kilometer	yr	year

Foreign and Scholarly Words

abr.	abridged, abridgment
ad lib. (*ad libitum*)	at will
anon.	anonymous
c. or ca. (*circa*)	about, approximately
cf. (*confer*)	compare
chap.	chapter
Cie (*Compagnie*)	Company
e.g. (*exempli gratia*)	for example
eq.	equation (pl., eqq. or eqs.)
esp.	especially
et al. (*et alii*)	and others
etc. (*et cetera*)	and so forth
et seq. (*et sequentes*)	and the following
f. or fem.	feminine; female
f.	and following (pl., ff.)
fig.	figure
gen.	genus; genitive
ibid. (*ibidem*)	in the same place
i.e. (*id est*)	that is
incl.	inclusive; including
inf. (*infra*)	below
infra dig. (*infra dignitatem*)	undignified
l.	line
lit.	literally
loc. cit. (*loco citato*)	in the place cited
m. or masc.	masculine
misc.	miscellaneous
m.m. (*mutatis mutandis*)	necessary changes being made
MS	manuscript (pl., MSS)
n. (*natus*)	born
N.B. (*nota bene*)	take careful note
non seq. (*non sequitur*)	it does not follow
ob. (*obiit*)	died
obs.	obsolete
op. cit. (*opere citato*)	in the work cited
p.	page (pl., pp.)
par.	paragraph
pass. (*passim*)	throughout; here and there

Foreign and Scholarly Words, cont.

pl.	plural; plate
pro tem (*pro tempore*)	for the time being
prox. (*proximo*)	next month
Q.E.D. (*quod erat demonstrandum*)	which was to be demonstrated
q.v. (*quod vide*)	which see
S.A. (*Société Anonyme*)	Corporation
ser.	series
sing.	singular
sup. (*supra*)	above
ult. (*ultimo*)	last month
v.	verse (pl., vv.), verso
v. (*vide*)	see
viz. (*videlicet*)	namely
vol.	volume
v. or vs. (*versus*)	against
v.s. (*vide supra*)	see above

Computers

Computer terminology makes heavy use of abbreviations. Commands, which differ in the various brands of software, are usually abbreviated and capitalized.

DIR (List Directory)	ERA (Erase)
STAT (check file length)	REN (rename a file)

The following list includes abbreviations that are frequently encountered in "computerese."

ADP	Automated Data Processing
ASCII	American National Standard Code for Information Interchange
BASIC	Beginners All-Purpose Symbolic Instruction Code
CD	Compact Disk
COBOL	Common Business Oriented Language
cpi	characters per inch
CP/M	Control Program for Microcomputers
cps	characters per second
CPU	Central Processing Unit
CRT	Cathode Ray Tube

DBMS	Data Base Management System
DMA	Direct Memory Access
DOS	Disk Operating System
DP	Data Processing
EDP	Electronic Data Processing
GIGO	Garbage In, Garbage Out
I/O	Input/Output
K, KB, or Kbyte	Kilobyte; 1,024 bytes
	(often rounded to 1,000 bytes)
LSI	Large Scale Integration
M, MB, or MByte	Megabyte; 1,048,576 bytes
	(often rounded to 1 million bytes)
MIS	Management Information System
Modem	Modulator-Demodulator
MS-DOS	MicroSoft Disk Operating System
OCR	Optical Character Recognition
PROM	Programmable Read-Only Memory
RAM	Random Access Memory
ROM	Read-Only Memory
UPS	Uninterruptable Power Supply
VDT	Video Display Terminal
VLSI	Very Large Scale Integration
WYSIWYG	What You See Is What You Get

CAPITALIZATION

Capital letters make a word stand out. To some extent, the words we capitalize reveal what we think is important or deserves emphasis. However, not everyone agrees on what is important, so there is conflicting advice about which words should be capitalized. I have drawn on modern authorities for the following guidelines, but I've tempered them with a few prejudices of my own.

A case in point is the word *federal*. The *Chicago Manual of Style* and *Words into Type* specify lowercase, unless the word is part of a proper name (Federal Trade Commission). *Success with Words* (published by Reader's Digest) and the *Government Printing Office Style Manual* capitalize *federal* (Federal government, Federal level, Federal agencies). My own sentiment is that the government is too godlike already without being further deified with a capital letter.

There are many such gray areas of capitalization. You have considerable latitude, as long as you are consistent. Keep track of which words you have capitalized on your style sheet.

A word processor makes changes in capitalization easy. Suppose you find an error or change your mind about whether to capitalize a given word. With Search and Replace and just a few keystrokes, the word processor will change the capitalization of the word every time it appears.

First Words

Capitalize the first word of a sentence.

> *A hospital should also have a recovery room adjoining the cashier's office.* — Francis O'Walsh

> Should the employees be notified? Which ones? How?

Capitalize the first word of a quotation.

> Gertrude Stein said, "Money is always there but the pockets change."

> "Only one fellow in ten thousand understands the currency question," according to Kin Hubbard, "and we meet him every day."

Notice the lowercase *a* in "and" in the above sentence.

Capitalize the first word of a saying or slogan.

> My grandmother used to tell me that Haste makes waste.

> A sign over the entrance reminds employees that Quality is up to us.

In numbered or outlined material, you can use caps or lowercase; whichever you choose, be consistent.

> Can we decide (a) when we will meet again? (b) what topics we will address?

> 1. Parts of Speech
>   a. noun
>   b. verb   *or*
>   c. adjective

> 1. Parts of Speech
>   a. Noun
>   b. Verb
>   c. Adjective

Capitalize the first word following a colon only if it begins a complete sentence.

> *There is just one thing I can promise you about the outer-space program: Your tax dollar will go farther.*—Wernher von Braun

> I suggest we adopt a new national flower: the concrete cloverleaf.

Capitalize the first word of a resolution:

> Resolved, That proliferation of nuclear weapons be halted ...
> Resolved by the city council, That ...

Titles, Headings, and Legends

Make the following *uppercase*:

• first and last words

> Words into Type

• all important words (nouns, pronouns, adjectives, adverbs, verbs, and subordinate conjunctions such as *although, because, since, unless, whether*)

> "I'll Be Seeing You"
> Legal Care for Your Software

• prepositions that are an inseparable part of a verb

> Fixing Up a Brownstone

• the first word of a hyphenated compound

> Defense Spending Re-examined

• the second word of a hyphenated compound if it's a noun or has the same force as the first word

> Cross-Country Skiing

Make the following *lowercase*:

• articles (a, an, the), unless they are the first word or follow a dash or colon

> How a First Book Became a Best-Seller
> In Search of Funding: A Quick Guide

- prepositions, unless they are the first or last word

> Writing with a Word Processor
> How to Succeed in Business without Really Trying
> For Whom the Bell Tolls

- the *to* in infinitives

> How to Write a Readable Business Report

- the second word of a hyphenated compound when it modifies the first word or when the words are considered a unit

> The Co-pilot's Handbook
> Free-for-alls in the Nation's Capital

Parts of a Book

The *Chicago Manual of Style* prescribes lowercase when referring to parts of a book or literary work: chapter 2, act 2, scene 2. *Words into Type* and *Success with Words* show uppercase as the correct treatment: Chapter 2. I prefer the capitalized version, because Chapter 2 seems like a proper noun (a specific chapter), and proper nouns are capped.

Passing reference to a table of contents, glossary, bibliography, and index appears in lowercase:

> In his introduction, Huxley states ...

but cross-references require capitals:

> Additional sources are listed in the Bibliography.

Names and Terms

Capitalize proper names or nouns (names of specific people or places):

> William Carlos Williams
> John F. Kennedy
> Washington, D. C.
> Shakespeare
> the Los Angeles Music Center
> the Astrodome
> Alexis de Tocqueville
> Wernher von Braun

Alexander the Great
Atlanta Braves
the Biltmore Hotel
Wild Bill Hickok
the Big Apple
American Telephone & Telegraph Company
Charles de Gaulle (but when the last name stands alone, DeGaulle)
First Lady Martha Washington (the First Lady)

Most words derived from proper nouns are lowercased.

arabic numerals
french fries
swiss cheese
venetian blinds
diesel engine
roman numerals
vulcanize
watt
klieg lights

Capitalize personal titles (professional, religious, military, and civil) that *immediately precede* a person's name.

President Washington
First Lady Martha Washington
Chief Justice Marshall
General Robert E. Lee
Sister Maria Constance
General Manager Garcia
Admiral Nancy F. Atherton
Rabbi Weiss
The Reverend Thomas Moore

Use lowercase when such titles are part of an appositive.

R. L. Knudsen, superintendent of schools
Alice Ramirez, vice-president of XYZ Corporation
Lee H. Howard, professor of astronomy
Woodrow Wilson, president of the United States from 1913 to 1921

the chairman of the Economics Department, Tilden F.
McCarthy
Canadian prime minister Leslie Latrelle
the governor of Nebraska

Also note the following usages:

the President, the Vice-President (when referring to the incumbent U.S. official)
the presidential yacht
the dean's office, the Dean's List
Fulbright scholar

Pardon me, Governor, will you make a statement?

The president of Techniplex will visit the company's Texas plant next week.

Geo-Political Terms

Words such as *state*, *avenue*, *city*, or *valley* are capitalized when they follow and are part of a specific name. They are usually lowercased when they precede the name or stand alone.

New York City, the city of New York
the Province of Quebec, the province
the Gulf Stream
the East, West, North, South (U.S.)
eastern time zone, southern accent, west of town, south of the border
southern Texas, upstate New York
Southern Hemisphere
the equator, the Equatorial Current
Long Island
a Carribbean island
the Australian Outback, the Outback
the Hawaiian Islands, one of the Hawaiian islands
the Islands, the Continent (when referring to a specific locale)
Mississippi River valley, the Mississippi Valley
Washington State, the state of Washington
Tenth Congressional District
John Hancock Building

the White House
the Fertile Crescent
Skid Row
Miracle Mile
the Versailles Treaty, the treaty of Versailles
Palos Verdes Peninsula (the proper name of a town), *but*
    the San Francisco peninsula (a general description)
Department of Defense, a defense contractor
Federal Aviation Administration
federal grant, federal employee
the Republican party, the Democrats, the Communist
    bloc, the Labor government
the Stone Age, the Jurassic period

Lowercase a plural generic term when it *follows* more than one name.

the John Hancock and Empire State buildings
the Missouri and Ohio rivers

Capitalize generic terms that *precede* more than one name.

Mounts McKinley and Ranier
Lakes Onandaga and Cayuga

Organizations, Institutions, Companies

Girl Scouts	Urban League
Humane Society	National Organization for Women
Scripps Institution	Metropolitan Museum of Art
Pomona College	Periwinkle Press
Stanford University	Society for the Preservation of Barber-Shop Quartets

Calendar

Capitalize days of the week, months, holidays (President's Day, Fourth of July), A.M., P.M. (small caps, if available; otherwise use lowercase: a.m., p.m.).

Lowercase seasons (spring, fall ...); time zones (central daylight time, Pacific standard time)

Religious Terms

Allah, Buddha, Elohim, Holy Father, Jesus Christ, the Messiah, Mohammed, the Supreme Being, Mater Dolorosa

Old Testament, the Koran, King James Version, Dead Sea Scrolls

Gnosticism, Sufi, Baha'i Faith, Presbyterian, Seventh-day Adventist

Ark of the Covenant, Garden of Eden, Ecce Homo, the Diaspora, the Crusades, the Hegira, the Inquisition

Scientific Terms

Genus is capitalized, species lowercased; both are set in italic type.

Homo sapiens

Larger divisions (phylum, class, order, family) are capitalized and set in roman type.

Chordata   Primates

English derivatives are lowercased.

primates   omnivores

Only proper names that are part of a medical term or physical law are capitalized.

Rhys' syndrome   Faraday's constant   Hodgkin's disease

The names of chemical elements and compounds are lowercased when written out; however, chemical symbols are capitalized.

sodium chloride   NaCl

Trademarks

The *Chicago Manual of Style* says "a reasonable effort" should be made to capitalize products that are protected by trademarks.

Seven-Up   Tylenol   Teflon   Kleenex   Xerox

Unless you have a reason for promoting a trademarked product, use generic terms where you can.

adhesive bandage, instead of Band-Aid
photocopy, instead of Xerox

On the other hand, whoever heard of an adhesive-bandage solution?

Military Terms

82nd Airborne Division
98th Field Artillery
Seventh Fleet, the fleet
United States Navy, the navy, the U.S. Navy, the U.S.S. New Jersey
Arkansas National Guard, the guard
Sergeant Willis Jones, the sergeant
the Allies, the Union soldiers, the Yankees, the Red Coats
Army headquarters
the Civil War
Napoleonic Wars
War of 1812
Victoria Cross
Purple Heart

Computers

Capitalization of computer terminology is in a state of flux. However, some conventions do seem to be consistently used. Most programming languages are all caps.

COBOL   BASIC   FORTRAN   PASCAL   Assembler

Computer functions (Search & Replace) or actions to be taken by an Operator (Save, Enter) are often given an initial cap.

Global Search   Insert Word   Delete Character
Write to File   Input from Keyboard   Goto

To some extent, you can write your own rules in this field, but be consistent. Keep track of such capital usage on your style sheet.

NUMBERS

The following rules will help you decide whether to express numbers as figures or words.

In business or technical writing or in journalism, use words for numbers 1 through 9; use figures for 10 or above.

> There were three applicants for the job.
> There were 12 applicants for the job.

In writing with a literary flavor, the dividing point is 100 instead of 10.

If a sentence or paragraph has related numbers that are both above and below 10, write the related numbers as figures.

> The three lines had 9, 10, and 11 applicants.
> > ("three" is not related to the other numbers and thus follows the previous rule)

Spell out numbers that begin a sentence; if a related number appears in the same sentence, write it as a word, too.

> Fifty million Frenchmen can't be wrong.
> Twenty members voted yes; fifteen voted no.
> > (*not* Twenty members voted yes; 15 voted no.)
> One dollar out of every ten earned in the U.S. goes into health care.

Express large numbers in figures or in mixed figure-word form; use whichever form you choose consistently.

> $10,000,000 or $10 million
> 5.7 billion
> 3½ million

Use figures for dates, as follows:

> July 4, 1976 *or* 4 July 1976
> 7/4/76 (U.S.)   4/7/76 (U.K.)
> > (Because of the confusion that might result from this form, writing the month as a word is preferred.)

Use figures with units of time or measurement:

10:00 a.m., 9 o'clock	2 half-gallons
32 degrees Fahrenheit	½-inch pipe
20 kilometers	8½ by 11 inch paper
3½ yards	55 MPH
6 acres	35-mm camera
3-foot ruler	a 40-hour week, *but* forty 20¢ stamps
1 × 8 inches	

Use figures in the following cases:

a vote of 5 to 4	an increase of 4.65
a score of 14-0	50 cents
a 3-for-1 stock split	a population of 10,372
divide by 2	Suite 1152

Use words in the following cases:

thousands of refugees
losses in the millions
twelve hundred words
a population of about fifty thousand
one-half of the work force
the Roaring Twenties
in their sixties *or* in their 60s

Commas

Americans and British use commas to separate long numbers into groups of three digits (10,576,435). The European practice calls for periods or spaces (4 000 000 or 4.000.000). Companies often have a style manual that dictates whether to use commas in a four-digit number that appears in the text (3,500 or 3500). In all cases, alignment of tabular matter requires commas when there are four or more digits.

3,500
17,100
619
6,800

Commas are not used in the following:

> page numbers (p. 1142)
> serial numbers (73027894WG)
> radio frequency (1330 kilocycles)
> to the right of the decimal point (1.53858)

Roman Numerals

Arabic numerals have replaced roman numerals in most situations. However, roman numerals are still used in prefatory matter (i, ii, iii, iv ...) and occasionally in copyright dates. Knowing how to translate them is sometimes useful. The rules are that a smaller number before a larger one *subtracts* from its value (XL = 40); a smaller number after a larger one *adds* to its value (LX = 60). Repeating a letter adds its value (XXX = 30). A bar over a numeral multiplies its value by 1,000 ($\overline{V}$ = 5,000; $\overline{M}$ = 1,000,000).

I = 1	C = 100
V = 5	D = 500
X = 10	M = 1,000
L = 50	

SPELLING

Misspelled words in business letters or manuscripts present your message in a flawed way. They also increase the likelihood of your being misunderstood and suggest that you are too lazy to look up the word in a dictionary.

Becoming a good speller is largely a matter of attitude. Once you are convinced that correct spelling is important, you will find the moments needed to look up and memorize difficult words. Make a list of the words that give you the most trouble, and update it as you master each one.

If a dictionary lists a second spelling, separated from the main entry by a comma or the word *or*, both spellings are considered acceptable (ax, axe). If the second spelling is separated by a period and introduced by the word *Also*, the main entry is preferred (esophagus.... Also oesophagus). Variant spellings also appear at their own alphabetical entry, labeled as variant (oesophagus, variant of esophagus); again, the main entry is preferred.

If you find a standard dictionary cumbersome, try using a "20,000 Words" type of reference. You lose some of the fringe benefits of a dictionary that way, but it is quicker. Spell-checking software that comes with most word processors provides a good backup.

The following guidelines focus on some of the most common spelling problems.

Suffixes

-ance or *-ence*

When the final *c* or *g* has a soft sound, use *-ence*, *-ent*, or *-ency.*

magnificent   emergency   indigent   obsolescence

When the final *c* or *g* has a hard sound, use *-ance*, *-ant*, or *-ancy.*

significant   extravagant

-able or *-ible*

Words that have an *-ation* form usually take *-able.*

dispensable (dispensation)   irritable (irritation)
quotable (quotation)   imaginable (imagination)

Words that have an *-ive, -tion, -sion,* or *-id* form usually take *-ible.*

combustible (combustion)   collectible (collective)
reversible (reversion)   digestible (digestion)

Exceptions: definable (definition), sensible (sensation)

-ceed, -cede, or *-sede*

Three words end with *-ceed* and one with *-sede.* All others ending in this syllable are spelled *-cede.*

exceed	supersede	accede
proceed		concede
succeed		precede
		secede, etc.

-ize or *-ise*

In general, this verb suffix is spelled *-ize* in the United States (ostracize, galvanize, pasteurize, sterilize) and *-ise* in the U.K. (ostracise, etc.) However, the preferred spelling in the U.S. of the following words is *-ise*:

advertise	exorcise
chastise	franchise

Some words in which the *-ise* ending is not a suffix but a part of the basic stem of the word are often misspelled.

enterprise	supervise
improvise	surprise

Adding Suffixes

When a word ends in a silent *e*, drop the *e* if the suffix begins with a vowel:

dance, dancing	smile, smiling
make, making	use, usable

Exceptions: mileage, shoeing, and words ending in a soft *c* or *g* (enforceable, manageable).

Retain the silent *e* if the suffix begins with a consonant:

grate, grateful	late, lately

Exceptions: abridgment, acknowledgment, awful, judgment, wholly, wisdom, and such words as duly and argument, in which the silent *e* is immediately preceded by a vowel other than *e*.

When a word ends in *ie*, change the *i* to *y* and drop the *e*.

die, dying	lie, lying

When a word ends with a *y* that is preceded by a vowel, retain the *y*.

buy, buyer   destroy, destroyer   enjoy, enjoyment

Exceptions: daily, gaiety, laid, paid, said

If the *y* is preceded by a consonant, change the *y* to *i* unless the suffix begins with *i*.

> body, bodily   dry, drier (i.e., more dry)
> happy, happiness

Exceptions: fryer, dryer (an appliance) and others formed from one-syllable words such as *shy* and *wry*; also, the words *baby, lady,* and the suffixes *-ship* (ladyship) and *-like* (citylike).

When a root word ends with a consonant that is preceded by a single vowel and the suffix begins with a vowel, double the consonant:

> allot, allotting   control, controlled
> forget, forgetting   occur, occurrence
> refer, referred   program, programmer
> regret, regrettable   remit, remittance
> transfer, transferring

Exceptions: buses, busing, transferable, and words where the accent moves from the last syllable to a preceding one (prefer, preference).

Do not double the final consonant if the suffix begins with a consonant:

> commit, commitment

if the final consonant is preceded by more than one vowel:

> congeal, congealed

or if the word is accented on any syllable except the last:

> bias, biased

Exceptions: handicapped, monogrammed, outfitter.

When the word ends in *c*, add a *k* in order to retain the hard sound:

> mimicking   picnicking   politicking   shellacked

Plurals

Most nouns are made plural by adding *s*:

alibis   beliefs   locks   values   paths   plaintiffs

or, if the word ends in *s, x, ch, sh,* or *j,* by adding *es*:

trenches   bushes   dresses   boxes

knife

If a noun ending in *y* is preceded by a consonant, change the *y* to *i* and add *es*:

cities   levies   countries   stories   families

Note: Proper names ending in *y* usually retain the *y* in their plural form.

both Germanys   the three Ogilvys

Exceptions: the Rockies, the Alleghenies

knives

Some nouns that end in *f, ff,* or *fe* are made plural by changing the *f* to *v* and adding *es*:

knives   shelves   halves   lives

Some of these have two forms:

scarves, scarfs   loaves, loafs   wharves, wharfs

If a noun ending in *o* is preceded by a vowel, add *s*:

cameos   ratios   studios   zoos

If the *o* is preceded by a consonant, an *es* is often added:

tomatoes   echoes   torpedoes   heroes

Some of the more than 40 exceptions to this rule are silos, commandos, mementos, and musical terms such as solos, banjos, and pianos.

Some nouns have the same form for singular and plural:

sheep   deer   corps
scissors   remains   offspring

Some nouns change internally to indicate the plural form:

tooth, teeth   mouse, mice   woman, women

Letters, acronyms, and numbers are usually made plural by adding *s* or *es*:

the 1980s   ABCs   at sixes and sevens   the three Rs

In abbreviations with periods or in words where adding *s* alone would be confusing, add *'s*:

R.N.'s   dotting your i's   too many why's

Make compound words plural by changing the principal word.

fathers-in-law   by-products   hangers-on
goose steps   sergeants-at-arms   notaries public

Hard-to-Spell Words

Many difficult words simply have to be memorized. However, once you decide to become a good speller, this is not hard to do. You soon develop a sense of whether a word "looks right." When in doubt, look it up.

The following words frequently show up on lists of spelling bugaboos.

accommodate
accumulate
acknowledgment
all right
consensus
embarrass
existence
harass
inoculate
iridescence
irrelevant
judgment
liaison

lightning
maintenance
maneuver
miscellaneous
parallel
prerogative
pseudonym
recommend
reconnaissance
renaissance
rhythm
surprise
weird

Compound Words

According to *The Chicago Manual of Style*, 9 out of 10 spelling questions concern compound words. Should you hyphenate a compound? write it as one word? two words? Even dictionaries don't agree on the treatment of many compounds, so keeping track of your decisions on a style sheet is essential.

The compound typically evolves in the following manner. First it appears as two words, called an open compound (hand gun). With increasing usage, it is hyphenated (hand-gun). When we see the elements as a single concept, they become one word and are called a closed compound (handgun).

In addition, compounds are considered "permanent" when they are an accepted part of our vocabulary and can be found in dictionaries. They are "temporary" when a writer joins the words for a specific, fleeting purpose (a divorce-prone millionaire).

The treatment of many compounds depends on their grammatical form (adjective, noun) and their position in a sentence (before or after a noun). A change in the order and form of words can create unit modifiers that require hyphens. Thus, *a citizen who abides by the law* becomes a *law-abiding citizen*. The words *law* and *abiding* have been moved in front of the noun *citizen*; the hyphen signals the reader that the words *law* and *abiding* are a single concept describing *citizen* (hence, a unit modifier). Individually they make no sense as modifiers (a law citizen, an abiding citizen). The hyphen turns the words into a useful, sensible modifier.

When a unit modifier is moved to a position following the noun, the individual words cease to function as a unit and the hyphen is omitted.

> The well-planned program ...
> The program was well planned.

> His company owns seven oil-drilling rigs.
> The company is engaged in oil drilling.

> The yet-to-be-heard-from senator ...
> The senator who is yet to be heard from ...

If the words making up the unit modifier remain changed in order or form when they follow the noun, retain the hyphen.

>These bonds are tax-exempt.
>>(These bonds are exempt from taxes.)

>Her response shows that she is a decision-maker.
>>(Her response shows that she is a person who makes decisions.)

The following list summarizes the more solid rules in the slippery world of compounding. Inevitably, some rules are followed by exceptions.

Spell the following compounds without hyphens:

• adverbs ending in *-ly*

>publicly held corporation   wholly owned subsidiary
>highly motivated reader   thoroughly understood gesture

• chemical terms

>amino acid mixture   carbon monoxide poisoning

• colors, if the first word modifies the second

>bluish green   lavender blue

but hyphenate if the elements are of equal importance

>blue-green algae   black-and-white photos

• proper names

>Civil War buff   New Age syndrome
>Central European countries

• foreign phrases, unless the phrase itself is hyphenated

>ad hoc committee   sub rosa payment
>*but* laissez-faire policy

• word describing relationship + noun

>sister city   foster parent
>parent model   fellow citizens

• temporary compounds formed with the word *master*

>master architect   master sculptor

but mastermind, masterpiece

- temporary compounds formed by a noun + gerund

    decision making   basket weaving   problem solving

but many permanent compounds are closed

    bookkeeping   winegrowing

- title + General

    Attorney General   Solicitor General

- *quasi* in noun form

    quasi victory   quasi corporation

- *vice* + title

The Chicago Manual of Style recommends hyphenating temporary compounds with *vice* (vice-chairman, vice-president) but spelling others as two words (vice admiral). Why *vice-president* is considered temporary and *vice admiral* permanent is not easy to see. According to the editors of *Success with Words*, the trend with *vice* compounds is away from the use of hyphens. They recommend choosing a specific dictionary as your guide and consistently following its treatment.

Hyphenate the following compounds:

- those beginning with *all, self, high,* or *low.*

    all-knowing   all-important   self-effacing
    self-seeking   high-energy physics   low-resolution screen

- those ending with *elect* and *designate*

    president-elect   senator-elect   ambassador-designate

but city clerk elect (and other offices consisting of two or more words)

- adjective-noun + *ed*

    quick-witted child   long-haired dog
    short-lived interest   hand-lettered sign
    growth-oriented company

- noun + present participle when appearing before a noun

    young-looking manager   bone-chilling effect
    time-consuming operation   thought-provoking statement

but Her statement was thought provoking.

- adverb-participle

    well-known principle   ill-advised plan
    much-loved friend   still-active volcano

but The volcano is still active.

- all *-in-laws* and *great-* relatives

    sister-in-law   great-uncle   great-great-grandfather

- number + *odd*

    twenty-odd   500-odd

- phrases used as adjectives

    soon-to-be-released film   better-late-than-never attitude
    cat-that-swallowed-the-canary smile

- *quasi* in adjective form

    quasi-public corporation   quasi-logical response

- noun + noun

    preacher-evangelist   statesman-scholar

- cardinal number + unit of measurement

    four-minute mile   30-yard line   12-volt battery

Spell the following compounds as one word:

- words ending in *-hood*, *-ache*, or *-fold*

    manhood   parenthood   heartache   toothache
    fortyfold   tenfold   *but* 10-fold

- words ending in *-like*, *-wide*, or *-book*, unless unwieldy

    statesmanlike   diamondlike   statewide   citywide
    textbook   checkbook   workbook

Exception: temporary compounds such as art book, photo book

Be alert to the constantly growing ranks of closed compounds, as frequent use turns temporary compounds into permanent ones.

> bestseller   childbearing   taxpayer   lifesaving

Also be aware of compounds whose meaning changes with a change in form.

> Anyone may attend.
> Any one of the books may be chosen.

> He stepped onto the stage.
> She went on to win the election.

The overriding consideration is to make the reader's job easier by making your meaning clear.

WORD DIVISION

Hyphenating words at the right-hand margin makes reading more difficult, so you want to do it as little as possible. But breaking up words is inevitable when the margins are justified and is highly likely even with unjustified material. Here are a few rules to tell you where to divide with a minimum of disruption for the reader.

Word Division Do's

Divide between syllables, according to pronunciation.

> market-able, not mar-ketable   dis-tant, not dist-ant

Divide between two consonants that are surrounded by vowels.

> mas-ter   phar-macy   sur-vey   sus-tain

Divide after a vowel unless such a division is not according to pronunciation.

> logi-cal, not log-ical   emi-grant, not em-igrant
> preju-dice, not prej-udice

> *but* trag-edy, not tra-gedy   antag-onize, not antago-nize

Divide at prefixes or suffixes that contain three or more letters.

> pre-ven-tion   super-market   infra-red
> contra-band   mother-hood   pseudo-science

Divide between doubled consonants unless they are at the end of the root word.

com-mit-tee   book-keeper   but-ter   can-non

but forestall-ing, not forestal-ling

Divide before *-ing*.

bill-ing   send-ing   think-ing   work-ing   know-ing

If the final consonant is doubled by adding *-ing*, carry the doubled consonant over to the next line.

recur-ring   swim-ming   run-ning   plan-ning

Divide hyphenated compounds at existing hyphens.

mother-in-law, *not* mo-ther-in-law
self-sufficient, *not* self-suf-ficient
lighter-than-air, *not* light-er-than-air

Word Division Don'ts

Don't divide one-syllable words.

thought   screamed   lounge   noise   burned   dumped

Don't divide one-letter syllables.

omen, not o-men   alive, not a-live   folio, not foli-o

Don't divide in such a way that you create a misleading pronunciation.

dancing, not danc-ing   subtle, not sub-tle
pred-ator, not pre-dator   hoping, not hop-ing

Don't divide the following word endings:

-cial, -sial, -tial, -cion, -gion, -sion, -tion, -ceous, -cious, -tious, -geous, -gious

Don't divide the syllables of a prefix.

micro-surgery, not mi-crosurgery
contra-indicated, not con-traindicated

Don't carry a two-letter syllable over to the next line.

leader, not lead-er   fainted, not faint-ed
friendly, not friend-ly

Don't carry over to the next line final syllables with an "ull" sound.

> people, not peo-ple   syl-lable, not sylla-ble
> mantle, not man-tle

Don't separate abbreviations and figures.

> 200 B.C., not 200/B.C.   1:00 a.m., not 1:00/a.m.
> 150 km, not 150/km

Don't divide personal names, if you can help it. If necessary, break after the middle initial.

> Phyllis O./Johnson   T.S./Eliot
> Samuel R. Towers,/Jr. but not Samuel R. Towers/III

Don't separate the elements of an outline or list, such as (a) or (1), from what follows them; carry such marks over to the next line rather than end the line with them.

Wrong: The program to redevelop the inner city will include (a) an environmental impact report, (b) sources of funding....

Right: The program to redevelop the inner city will include (a) an environmental impact report, (b) sources of....

Don't divide numbers. If you must, break at a comma but not at a decimal point.

> 10,/000,/000 $346,/521.83 but not $346,521./83

Don't divide the last word of more than two consecutive lines. Don't divide the last word of a paragraph or the last word on a right-hand page.

DOCUMENT INTEGRITY

Seemingly trivial errors in assembling a document turn your readers' attention to your incompetence instead of your ideas. A document may be 99 percent error-free, but it's the 1 percent that gets noticed.

The changes made during editing increase the possibility of a mismatch between parts of a document. Gaps in numbering, missing figures or tables, and discrepancies between the Table of Contents and text are typical slip-ups. Edit for this kind of integrity with a separate pass through a document, checking the following elements.

Numbering. Are pages, sections, and chapters numbered sequentially? Are cross-references correct? Are references to other documents numbered sequentially and listed in that order in a bibliography?

Figures and Tables. Are figures and tables numbered sequentially? Is the numbering style consistent (e.g., arabic or roman numerals, hyphenation, decimals)? Is the format and style of captions uniform? Are the titles or captions of any figures or tables identical? If so, change them so that readers can distinguish between them.

Table of Contents. Does the text for all of the headings cited still exist? Are the headings correctly worded? Are the page numbers correct?

Page Layouts. Do running heads (chapter or section titles that appear at the top of each page) match the text? Are numbered footnotes sequential?

Parallelism. Is every subparagraph (a) followed by subparagraph (b)? Is (i) followed by (ii)?

Cross-References. Are all the numbers that are cited correct (page, paragraph, section, chapter)? Have deletions left a cross-reference stranded?

DOCUMENT APPEARANCE

A reader's first impression of what you have written is visual. Is it pleasing to the eye? Keep the goal of a visually strong presentation in mind as you make decisions about a document's appearance.

If you have a word processor, you have many options: justified right-hand margins, the amount of space between characters and between lines, boldface type, and so on. The type of document (or in-house policy) may determine these choices. If not, experiment to find what works best.

Spacing is a key ingredient. Information is more readily absorbed if it isn't too densely packed, so create plenty of white space around your words by allowing ample margins.

Indented portions of text and bulleted information are eye-catching, and an outline format is occasionally useful to emphasize the organization of your material. However, avoid indenting so many times that the text is squeezed into the right side of the page.

Should you add chapter headings? section headings or footings? They can help the reader find a specific part of a long document. Location of page numbers is another variable. Which looks best: top or bottom of the page, centered or at the margin, alternate numbers on the left and right margins of facing pages? Try several locations and decide.

Are the page breaks satisfactory? Printers advise you to avoid the following "bad breaks."

- a short line (a "widow") at the top of a page

- a heading at the bottom of a page
(at least two lines of text should follow a heading)

- a page that ends with a hyphenated word
(some accept such a break on a left-hand page)

- a quoted portion that begins on the last line or ends on the first line of a page (at least two lines of the quotation should appear in either place)

- a footnote that is not on the same page as its original citation (if the first two lines are on the same page, the footnote can be continued on the following page)

As you look at the appearance of the final document, divorce yourself from its content and consider only its visual impact. If the document is attractive, you're off to a good start with the reader.

Chapter 9

Computer-Age Writing

Chapter 9.
COMPUTER-AGE WRITING

From note-taking and first drafts to the final polished copy, word processors provide today's writers with a dazzling array of ways to improve writing. The most dramatic is the ease of revising. No more scissors and tape, no more "white out," no more tedious retyping of entire documents. Instead, inserting and deleting text, rearranging paragraphs or whole sections, changing formats, and printing clean drafts—all are quickly done with a word processor. Last-minute rewrites that were previously considered too expensive and time-consuming are now practical.

In fact, you might get the impression that today's word processing software can do the whole editing job. Wrong. A grammar-checker can catch certain kinds of errors, and a spelling-checker is a must for chronic misspellers. But such programs are limited. Let's look at just what grammar- and spell-checking programs will and won't do for you.

Grammar-Checkers

In the plus column, the grammar-checker identifies certain words as archaic, awkward, vague, or sexist. It stops at pairs of words that are commonly misused (*affect* and *effect*) and provides definitions so you can confirm that you've chosen the right one. It identifies certain redundant, overworked, wordy, or trite phrases. It points out where you've used a trademark (*Coke, Xerox*), an "informal" word (*ain't*), or a form of the verb *to be* (a warning that you may be using the passive voice); it helps you detect noun-heavy writing by counting prepositions.

A grammar-checker catches doubled punctuation marks (,,), doubled words (the the), and doubled capital letters (WOrd). It points out missing spaces after punctuation marks (red,white). It checks whether you've used both opening and closing quotation marks, parentheses, and other marks that should appear as pairs. It warns you of overworked words by listing them according to the number of times they appear.

The grammar-checker helps you determine if your writing is readable by listing the number of sentences, number of words, average sentence length, and average word length. It counts the words in the shortest and longest sentences and identifies both. Some programs will calculate the school grade level needed to read the document.

All this might make the life of the editor sound pretty easy. Some might conclude that knowing how to edit is as useful as knowing how to start your car with a crank. But consider what grammar-checking software can't do, as well as a few of the things it does that you wish it didn't.

A grammar-checker won't find ambiguous words or incomplete sentences. It can't distinguish between verbs and nouns, so it can't tell if your subjects and verbs agree. It doesn't know where to put commas or apostrophes. It won't tell you which words to capitalize other than "I" and the first word of a sentence. It doesn't force you to think about your audience or the logic behind your presentation. It doesn't catch faulty references or misplaced modifiers.

If your text includes non-standard sentences, the analysis of sentence length is thrown off. For example, this book contains lists and examples that are preceded by a colon. My grammar-checker counts each as a sentence, thereby identifying some 147-word "sentences."

Grammar-checkers have a restricted view of certain words, such as *rather*. They don't distinguish between proper use of the word (*I would rather be right than be President.*—Henry Clay) and sloppy usage (The speech was rather long). They would criticize its use in the following as "a vague adverb."

> *I never saw a Purple Cow,*
> *I never hope to see one;*
> *But I can tell you, anyhow,*
> *I'd rather see than be one.*
> —Gelett Burgess

My grammar-checker will advise me to substitute *very* for *awfully*, then rap my knuckles if I follow its advice (*very* is another "vague adverb"). I agree that *awfully* is an inelegant word and that *very* is a vague adverb, but better advice would simply be "revise."

The grammar-checker's mindlessness can be tedious. You will be accused of sexism whenever you write "his" or "she," even though the accusation may be unfounded. And if you know the correct use of such words as *affect* and *effect*, you may be annoyed by being reminded of their meaning each time they appear.

A grammar-checker is probably worth the price just for its ability to analyze word and sentence length. It's also useful as a proofreading backup, catching errors that human eyes occasionally miss. But much of the information it provides is useful only if you know how to apply it; it's no substitute for good judgment and a knowledge of the fundamentals of writing and editing.

Spell-Checkers

Software that catches misspelled words is a great help for people who are poor spellers, but it, too, has irritating characteristics. Since the spell-checker assumes that any word it doesn't recognize is misspelled, it mistakenly flags many correct words. Names, acronyms, compound words, and hyphenated words are usually treated as misspelled. You can alleviate this nuisance by adding frequently used proper names or acronyms to the spell-checker's vocabulary. Thereafter, these words will be recognized as correct.

Spell-checkers assume that if a word is correctly spelled, it is the correct word. You may have chosen the wrong word, but the spell-checker will not call it to your attention. For example, if you write *their* as *thier*, the spell-checker will point out your error. But if you spell it *there*, your mistake will go unnoticed since you have used a real—though incorrect—word. Careful proofing with a dictionary and a list of of the words you often misspell is still necessary. (Some simple rules to help you become a better speller are presented in Chapter 8.)

Putting Your System to Work

In the following pages I explore some of the ways to use a word processor when writing and editing. Your system may not have all of the functions I refer to; it may have others I don't mention. But whether it's simple or sophisticated, your word processor is much more than a fancy typewriter. Learn how it can help you do a better job.

Re-read your Operator's Manual occasionally. Instructions that previously seemed to be written in an esoteric code may become clear in time. You'll discover tricks that you didn't notice when struggling to master the fundamentals. If your word processor still lacks important features, you might want to acquire additional software or replace your system with a state-of-the-art model.

The word processing jargon in the pages that follow will probably differ from some of the terms used in your manual. One software writer's Search and Replace is another's Find and Insert, but the drift should be clear. The terms I use describe operations or functions that you or the system perform: Save, Copy, Global Search, and so on. Since most of these words are found in our everyday vocabulary, I have adopted the common practice of capitalizing to alert you to the special use of an ordinary word.

Writing

Word processors have blurred the distinction between writing and editing. The once sharply defined steps of writing, analyzing, and revising can now be integrated into a more smoothly flowing whole: you revise as you write, and write as you revise. You can be more daring and experimental—even more exhaustive—knowing that you can easily make changes later.

The First Draft. Some writers still swear by their yellow lined pads or their favorite ballpoint pen for the first draft. They find the creative juices respond more readily to a certain comfortable chair, or they prefer to make the first major shufflings with paper instead of electronics. But other writers find that they are more productive when the first draft is written on a word processor. A blank screen somehow seems less intimidating than a blank piece of paper.

The ease of making changes frees you from concern about how many drafts you will go through. Instead of starting the editing process in your head in order to minimize retyping, your fingers quickly transform thoughts into words that you can see. Ideas are not lost while you struggle for the "perfect phrase."

> *Thinking is the activity I love best, and writing to me is simply thinking through my fingers.*—Isaac Azimov

The very act of quickly putting the material in visible form helps sort it out. You can see that one idea is more important than another, that a good opening line is buried in the third paragraph, and so on.

If you are stumped for a specific word or phrase, mark the spot with a non-printing marker or a distinctive key (like © or @). Later, use Search to locate those markers; by then you may have thought of the right word. Or perhaps you have several candidates for the "right word." Put them all in, mark them with brackets, and recall them later with Search. The choice will probably be easier when you've let some time elapse. Unless you used non-printing markers, you must remember to remove the markers when you've made your choice. The thesaurus that comes with many word processors simplifies the search for "the right word."

Speed. Whether you're taking notes or making the last change in wording, a word processor speeds up the job. Typing is faster with the quiet keyboard and Word Wrap. No more bells that ring at the end of a line, no more Margin Release Key to press so that you can squeeze in one more word. You just type and type.

Typing is also faster with Programmable Function Keys (macros) and Phrase Storage (Glossary). With these capabilities you can store frequently used commands or long words and phrases that will appear in the text. When you want those words or phrases typed, or when you want certain commands performed automatically, all you have to do is press a key or two. The word processor types the words or performs the command for you. For example, a typical signature block might have 75 characters.

Very truly yours,

NEW HORIZONS INVESTMENT COUNSELORS

Tracy W. Thompson

Tracy W. Thompson
Vice-President

It takes 2 keystrokes instead of 75 when the signature block is stored in a macro or the Glossary.

Standard letter closings, long titles, or frequently used phrases can also be stored in this way. A log is essential to keep track of the words and phrases you've stored.

If your software doesn't have programmable keys or a Glossary, you might want to devise your own. Establish a code based on infrequently used keys (>, ©, or +) or doubled keys that don't appear as such in the text (## or }}), and type the code in place of each name or phrase. When you have completed the first draft, use Search and Replace to change ">" to "Sir William Fitzhugh-Blennerhasset" or " + " to the "post hoc ergo propter hoc fallacy"—or whatever. If you prefer, simply abbreviate and later change the abbreviations to the complete words with Search and Replace (e.g., "CD" becomes "Certificates of Deposit").

Revising

The descriptive word for revising with a word processor is EASIER. Insertions are easier, deletions are easier, moving sections around is easier, and working with clean, newly printed copies is gloriously easier. Just as the word processor allows you to write boldly and freely, it also helps you edit more thoroughly. No longer do revisions have to be *really important* to make retyping worthwhile. Even minor changes can be justified because making them and printing a new copy is so simple. No longer does revising feel like a punishment—playing with the text can be fun.

Perform your first rough editing on the display screen. This cleans up long documents and makes revising the hard copy easier. Short documents that you've edited on the screen may survive with no further editing.

As you experiment with different wordings, don't destroy earlier versions until you're sure you're abandoning them. If you have a new idea for a beginning, type it directly below your original one and evaluate the two approaches with a one-on-one comparison. Split screens or windows are helpful but not essential. If the portions you are comparing will not all fit on the screen, print them and compare the hard copies. When you have decided which is best, discard the unused portion. Print copies of each version if you want a paper trail of the document's evolution.

If you expect to perform major surgery on the document, first Copy the sections you will be working on. This insures that you still have the original version to fall back on if your experiments produce a monster. If the experiments succeed, replace the original with the new text.

I find that printing hard copies is essential to the editing process. Although I make plenty of changes on the screen, I like to see how the words look on paper. A hard copy reveals the flow in a way that screenfuls of text cannot. Spreading the pages on a table is also helpful. It allows me to view them in one sweep and take a first cut at a major rearrangement of sections.

Use bold colors to mark changes on the hard copy. In the days when retyping was a chore, unobtrusive corrections helped you get more mileage out of a given draft. Now what's important is to make your changes easy to see as your eyes move back and forth between paper and screen.

You might find an "orphan file" a useful concept. As you edit, you invariably toss out large chunks of writing. They may be gems, but for some reason they don't fit in the project at hand. Save these deleted portions in an orphan file. Your golden prose may yet have a use, if you've stored it where it can be retrieved.

Typeover vs. Insert. Is it more efficient to use Typeover or Insert when making changes in a word or sentence? It's my experience that trying to salvage bits and pieces of text takes more time than using Insert to type a new version and then Delete to remove the unwanted portion. I'll illustrate with a simple revision.

To change: one of the main features
to: a main feature

INSERT METHOD:
Move the cursor to the letter "o"
In the Insert mode, type "a main feature"
Delete "one of the main features"

TYPEOVER METHOD:
Move the cursor to the letter "o"
In the Typeover mode, type "a"
Delete "ne of the"
Move cursor to "s"
Delete "s"

When you Typeover, you have to be careful not to gobble up letters or words you want to save. You must move the cursor over those parts, Typeover until you come to other parts you want to save, change to Insert if you run out of space to Typeover, move the cursor again, and so on. It takes longer to figure out where to move the cursor and how many strokes to Typeover before changing to Insert than it does simply to type the new word or phrase.

Overtyping is useful for simple spot corrections, like changing "hte" to "the" or transposing identical words (changing "she only read" to "she read only)." But if you have to stop to think whether the entire correction can be made with Typeover, you've already lost too much time. You're better off staying keyed into the Insert mode, and using Insert/Delete as your standard method of correction. If you're bothered by seeing the line of type jiggle in front of you when you're Inserting text, add a couple of blank lines ahead of your insertion. Remember to remove them later.

Using Search and Replace. The Search and Replace function is a powerful tool in the editor's repair kit. Among others, it can help you perform the following functions:

- correct repeated errors with one entry
- check usage or punctuation
- correct or update information
- locate portions of the text for revision
- create an index
- change format
- insert cross-references

The same error made repeatedly, such as the misspelling of a name, can be corrected in one quick pass through the document with Global Replace. Or suppose you decide to change "apartment" to "condominium" or "secretary" to "administrative assistant." Each use of the original term is found and replaced, but you only had to type the replacement term once. Selective Replace shows you each occurrence of the word or phrase you specify. It then gives you the option of making a correction or of leaving the text unchanged and moving on to the next occurrence of the "Search String."

Sophisticated word processors can ignore the distinction between uppercase and lowercase letters as you make changes with Search and Replace. Thus, if your Search String is "theatre," the word

"I think you should trade your word processor in for a trash compactor."

processor will recognize it in both upper and lowercase forms (theatre, Theatre, or THEATRE). Furthermore, it will retain the case it finds as it makes the changes you specify (theater, Theater, or THEATER). If your word processor isn't case-sensitive in this way, omit the initial capital letter when you identify the word to Search for. Typing "heatre" will locate both "theatre" and "Theatre."

If you ask the word processor to Search for a short word that happens to be part of another word, you may waste time with irrelevant words found by the system. For example, a Search for the word "is" will also locate "this," "mishap," "isopropyl," and "Mississippi." You can avoid this nuisance by specifying "whole words only" or by typing Hard Spaces around the letters or word you are asking the system to find.

Search and Replace makes cross-references easy to handle. In the first draft, type one, two, or three Xs wherever you cite page numbers (based on your estimate of the ultimate number of digits in the citation). When the final draft is complete, locate each cross-reference with Search; Replace the Xs with the correct page number.

Searching with key words can help you locate sections of text that you want to revise. For example, if you want to update the parts of a document that relate to taxes, creating a Search String with such key words as "tax," "assessment," "withholding," "tariff," or "IRS" will lead you to the relevant text.

Sometimes you can combine Searches by using a single Search String to look for several problems. For example:

Search String	Potential Problems
-ing	dangling participle, sentence fragment, idea subordination, possessive with gerund
that	faulty reference, sentence fragment, that/which choice
and	parallel construction, monotonous sentence structure
it	faulty reference, agreement, weak sentence opening
which	punctuation of restrictive/non-restrictive clauses, faulty reference, that/which choice
forms of "to be"	passive voice, drab style
who	faulty reference, subject or object, who/whom choice

Thus, by defining your Search String as the word *who*, you can check at the same time whether the antecedent of the word is clear, and whether you have used the correct case (should it be "who" or "whom"?).

Marking the Manuscript for Search. A marking system can simplify your Search procedure. Mark the text with one kind of symbol to show where you've omitted information, another to direct you to a passage that needs rewriting. Use distinctive marks for key words or headings as the first step in compiling an index or table of contents. Mark cross-references in the first draft to make them easier to find when you're ready to insert the correct page numbers in the final version.

Non-printing remarks are a convenient way to mark a manuscript. Since they show only on the screen and not on the hard copy, you don't have to remove them before printing. If your word processor doesn't have non-printing comments, you can create your own marking system with doubled keys (++) or symbols you haven't used in the text (©). When these marks have served their purpose, however, you must remove them before printing the final copy.

Regardless of what kind of marking system you use, a record of the way you use each symbol helps keep track of your coding: one symbol for key words, one for missing information, another for rewrites, and so on. This allows you to move directly (with Search) to the desired place in the text.

Watch Out! A hazard in revising with a word processor is that you fail to catch all the loose ends created by changes you've made. If you use Search and Replace to change "I" to "we," you must also change related verbs from singular to plural. A new location for a sentence may result in two consecutive sentences beginning with "Although." Changing verb tense requires you to pursue the ripple effect in the adjoining material; do those verbs need to be changed, too? An incomplete deletion can leave a stray word in the middle of a sentence or a sentence fragment in the middle of a paragraph. Be especially alert for such loose ends when proofreading.

The very ease of writing with a word processor can be a danger. Having made it so effortless to generate words, your word processor must now be used to trim the excess. Tighten your prose by energetically removing rambling sentences or repetitious thoughts. (See p. 66, Trim the Lard.)

> ... *word processors can be responsible for producing a good deal of flabby writing. The words come out of you like toothpaste sometimes. There's no shortage of sheer wordage in America; more sentences are not what this country needs.*
> —Garrison Keillor

Formatting

With a typewriter, formatting consists largely of setting the right and left margins, determining how far down the page to start typing, and choosing single, space-and-a-half, or double spacing. With a word processor, you have many more choices. Do you want the right-hand margin justified? A brief command and it's done. Do you want to squeeze the text because of space considerations? Maybe you'd rather stretch it out for easy reading? You can do either with a format command that specifies the amount of space between letters. You can also set the space between lines in smaller increments than are available on typewriters. You can establish standard blocks of text at the top or bottom of each page (headers or footers) and make page numbering automatic and flexible.

Format commands can be changed to fit changing needs. For example, when writing drafts you should allow plenty of space between lines for corrections and perhaps an extra wide margin on one side for reviewers' comments. You might indent the first line of paragraphs to make them easier to locate. But when it comes to the final version, you need to tighten up the layout. With revised commands, you can change to conventional spacing and margins. Search and Replace removes indentations you no longer want by Searching for five spaces and Replacing them with zero spaces.

On certain word processors, the display screen shows how the printed page will look. With this what-you-see-is-what-you-get type of word processor, underlined portions are actually underlined, justified text appears justified, and boldface words are boldfaced. The lengths of the lines on the screen are just as they will be when printed. This allows you to correct any unsatisfactory line breaks by hyphenating words or rewording to make line spacing appropriate. In other words, you can pretty much design the printed page on the screen.

If your display only approximates how the printed page will look, some educated guesses and a hard copy will determine whether format corrections are needed. Most word processors at least show you where page breaks will occur. This enables you to avoid undesirable page endings, such as a heading stranded without its accompanying text.

Check page breaks before you print, and make changes where appropriate. If a heading or the first line of a paragraph has been separated from the text that follows it, use Page Break to force the page to end at the close of the previous paragraph. This will reunite the heading or first line and the subsequent text on the next page.

If only the final line of a paragraph has been carried over to the top of a page, set Page Break a line or two above the final line. This will force the word processor to carry over at least two lines of text to the next page. If your word processor has "Widow and Orphan" protection, all of this can be done automatically.

Standard Formats. Different kinds of documents have different layouts. Memos, letters, reports, quotations, and press releases all have a distinctive arrangement of margins, spacing, indentation, and page length. You can avoid typing format commands every time you start a new File by creating a macro for each format. You can also establish each frequently used layout as a separate File. These Files could include such specifications as margins, line spacing, indentations, justification, running headers or footers, proportional spacing, tabs, page numbering, or multiple columns. You might also want to include standard headings for memos, press releases, or certain types of reports (e.g., monthly sales reports).

Let's use a memo as an example. First establish the desired memo format with your layout commands. You might specify four lines per inch, a top margin of two inches, bottom margin of one inch, right and left margins of one-and-a-half inches, and standard headings such as To, From, Subject, and Date. Name this standard format MEMO and Save it. Then Copy this File; you now have two identical Files consisting solely of the format layout line and headings. Type your message in the duplicate of MEMO, and Save it under a File name that is chosen to reflect its contents. The properly formatted, completed memo is now stored as a separate File, and the original File, MEMO, remains available for future memos by repeating this procedure. Any frequently used format lends itself to this approach. If you wish, you can establish separate Files for long and short memos or letters; S-MEMO could specify the layout command for short (half-size) pages and L-MEMO for long (full-size) pages.

File Management

Learning how to manage disk Files takes a while, and developing systematic procedures is essential. But you can store an astonishing amount of information in a small space, and you won't get hangnails in the process.

It helps to indicate when a diskette is formatted and ready for use by placing a small symbol in one corner of the label. Putting a stripe of color with a marking pen across the top of the label further identifies the diskette; for example, green for backups, red for programs, blue for correspondence. You can color code to identify authors, where more than one person uses a system, or to identify companies on which you keep extensive Files. Keep a written record of your color coding system, and *always* use felt-tipped rather than ballpoint pens when writing on diskette labels.

Leave some space in your Files instead of packing in all they will hold. You may want to add substantial portions later, and it's smart to save room for that possibility. Block Moves also require elbow room, since the word processor first copies the Block at its new location before allowing you to delete the original Block.

To break a long File, first create a new File to receive the part you are moving. Give it a name that reminds you of the connection between the two Files (such as adding X, 2, or CONT to the original File name). Then use Block Move to transfer part of the original File to the new File. Another approach is to Copy the entire File and then Delete the last half of one and the first half of the other. Rename the continuation File.

You should leave room for File manipulation on diskettes as well as within individual Files. For example, a grammar-checker needs space to copy an entire File before marking each error it finds. You avoid the inconvenience of a "Disk Full" warning if you allow for this kind of File juggling.

Nevertheless, there will probably be times when you try to store your latest work, only to be told the disk is full. The simplest remedy is to replace the diskette with a clean, formatted one. Save the revised document on the fresh diskette, and later remove the earlier version from the full diskette. Another approach is to Delete parts of the File that were not revised and later retrieve them from your

Backup. If all else fails, Print the part you have been unable to Save and retype it later.

How often should you Save what you are writing? Those who have lost hours of work when the system crashed or the power failed tend to be pretty conservative. Saving every 15 or 20 minutes, or every screenful, becomes a sacred ritual. If that seems excessive, make your criterion that you Save whenever you can't afford to lose what you've typed since the last Save.

Despite your best efforts, there may be times when you lose some text. Reconstruct it as best you can right away. You will probably be surprised by how much you remember—certainly much more than you'd remember if you put it off for an hour or a day.

The best cure of all, of course, is prevention. If you keep track of how much room is left in a File, restrict Files to a manageable size, Save frequently, and make Backups regularly, you will never have a Disk-Full problem.

Boilerplate. The first step in creating a boilerplate library is to write and Save a variety of standard paragraphs: responses to frequently asked questions, biographical sketches, descriptions of company policies or facilities, sales information, standard openings and closings. Number or name each paragraph for later retrieval. Type a Table of Contents at the beginning of each boilerplate File, adding as much descriptive detail as you need to identify each paragraph.

By Copying the paragraphs that apply to a given situation, you can piece together a new document. Skillful use of this word processing feature for letters, proposals, and press releases makes documents look freshly written despite their assembly-line production. Boiler-plate is also a timesaver in writing proposals and legal documents. But be sure the boilerplate paragraphs fit together smoothly, and revise any words or expressions that adjacent paragraphs have made repetitious.

> *Word carpentry is like any other kind of carpentry: You must join your sentences smoothly.*—Anatole France

Printing

The ease and speed of printing is a major attraction of writing with a word processor. Although editing on the display screen is a great boon to writers, having fresh copies—frequently—is an even greater one.

There is a danger that the newly printed page will make the writing look better than it actually is. The pristine appearance can mask the need for additional revision. But clean copies can also provide a new perspective on the basic structure of the writing. Somehow words and paragraphs look different when printed; flow, or the absence of it, becomes obvious. New approaches come to mind more readily when you see the words on a printed page. And hard copies are added insurance against that ultimate disaster: loss or destruction of a diskette. If you date and file the printed copies, you have a record of the evolution of your drafts.

If your word processor has Spooling, you can work on one document while the printer is printing another. This is a big help when you're facing a deadline, and it's generally a good way to increase efficiency. For example, when you have Entered and Saved the corrections on the first section of a long document, you can be printing it while making corrections in the second section. This section-by-section method is faster than editing the entire report and then waiting while it is printed.

Chain Printing hooks one document to another automatically. In effect you create one continuous document from sections that are stored as separate Files. Page numbers are sequential, and no visible signs reveal the separate origins of the Files. What *is* evident with Chain Printing is that you finish the task faster.

If your document will serve as camera-ready art for reproduction, you may want to print with Double Strike on coated paper. Double Strike produces a slightly darker image by causing the printer to hit the printing element twice for each letter. This also makes a stronger carbon copy. Boldface is even darker than Double Strike and emphasizes headings or words you want to stand out.

Other capabilities that come with many printers are <u>double underlining</u>, overstrike (~~overstrike~~) and strikeout (~~strikeout~~); the latter two are useful in legal documents or in editing someone else's writing on diskettes. Subscript and superscript are used in technical manuscripts for chemical formulas (H_2O) and for footnote numbers.[1]

Writing and editing with a word processor is a mixed blessing. A word processor can seduce you into wordiness, and it will probably increase the appearance of stray words and sentences that were created during revisions. But the source of the illness also provides the cure. Word processors speed up, simplify, and improve writing in ways that have not been possible before; they have become indispensable in the writer-editor's armamentarium.

---

[1]Footnote

Glossary

Adjective. A word that describes or limits the meaning of a noun or noun phrase.

Niagara Falls is simply a vast unnecessary amount of water going the wrong way and then falling over unnecessary rocks. —Oscar Wilde

Adverb. A word that modifies or expands the meaning of a verb, adjective, or other adverb.

... there is no distinctively native American criminal class except Congress. —Mark Twain

Alliteration. The use of words that begin with or contain the same letter or sound, in order to achieve a certain effect.

Finding Facts Fast
Write Right! A Desk Drawer Digest ...

Antecedent. The word, phrase, or clause referred to by a pronoun. Skilled writers avoid ambiguous antecedents. (See p. 57 and p. 117.)

I'm a great believer in luck, and I find that the harder I work the more I have of it. —Thomas Jefferson

Antonym. A word having a meaning opposite to the meaning of another word. (See Synonym.)

slow/fast   hot/cold   difficult/easy

Appositive. A noun or phrase that identifies the preceding word or concept.

Gabriel Garcia Marquez, the Nobel laureate, ...
my supervisor, Jack Bowman, ...

Article. The word *a, an,* or *the.* Usually classified as adjectives.

Case. The inflection or change made to a pronoun in order to show its relation to other words. Pronouns in the *nominative* (also known as *subjective*) case are subjects of sentences (*we*), in the *objective* case are objects of verbs or prepositions (*us*) and in the *possessive* case show possession (*our*).

> We gave them our answer.

We is the subject of the verb *gave,* *them* is its object, and *our* shows possession of the noun *answer.*

Clause. A group of words that contains a subject and predicate.
An *independent clause* expresses a complete thought.
A *dependent (subordinate) clause* does not express a complete thought and depends on the main (independent) clause to complete its meaning.

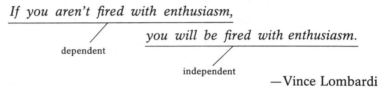

> *If you aren't fired with enthusiasm,*
>   dependent
>   *you will be fired with enthusiasm.*
>   independent
>   —Vince Lombardi

A *restrictive clause* is necessary to define or limit the word it modifies; it is not set off by commas.

> *My clothes are addressed to women who can afford to travel with forty suitcases.*—Yves Saint Laurent

A *nonrestrictive clause* adds information but does not limit what it modifies; it is set off by commas.

> *To say nothing, especially when speaking, is half the art of diplomacy.*—Will and Ariel Durant

Cliché. An expression that was once fresh but has become dull and stereotyped by overuse.

> Clichés should be avoided like the plague.

Complement. A word or phrase that completes the meaning of the verb.

> The judge named Sanchez jury foreman.
> We found their argument unconvincing.

> *Happiness is having a scratch for every itch.*—Ogden Nash

> If I'd known I was going to live so long, I'd have taken better care of myself.—Leon Eldred

Compound. Consisting of two or more elements.

> *How can one conceive of a one-party system in a country that has over two hundred varieties of cheese?*—Charles deGaulle
> (compound adjective)

> *The wisdom of the wise and the experience of the ages are perpetuated by quotations.*—Benjamin Disraeli
> (compound subject)

> *I hate and regret the failure of my marriages.*—J. Paul Getty
> (compound verb)

Compound words are classified as follows:

A *temporary compound* consists of words joined by the writer for a momentary purpose.

> *Love is a many-splintered thing.*—R. Buckminster Fuller

A *permanent compound* can be found in the dictionary, indicating its acceptance in our language: half-breed.

An *open compound* is written as two separate words: cash crop.

A *closed compound* is written as a single word: casework, paycheck.

Conjunction. A word that connects words, phrases, and clauses. *Coordinating conjunctions* (*and, but, or, nor, for, yet,* and *so*) connect elements of equal rank:

> nuts *and* bolts   Tom, Dick, *or* Harry

Two independent clauses are joined by a coordinating conjunction:

> *Music is my mistress, and she plays second fiddle to no one.*
> —Duke Ellington

> *Civilization is unbearable, but it is less unbearable at the top.*—Timothy Leary

Coordinating conjunctions used in pairs are called *correlatives*:

> either/or   not only/but also   both/and

Subordinating conjunctions (*that, when, where, while, if, because, although, since,* etc.) connect elements of unequal rank (i.e., an independent and a dependent clause).

> *A man in love is incomplete <u>until</u> he has married. Then he's finished.*—Zsa Zsa Gabor

Contraction. The use of an apostrophe to indicate omitted letters or numbers.

> <u>can't</u> for <u>cannot</u>   '50 for 1950

Dangling Modifier. A modifier that cannot logically modify any word in a sentence. (See p. 122.)

> Having left in a hurry, his wallet was still on the dresser.

Gerund. A verb form that ends in *-ing* and is used as a noun. (See Participle.)

> Debugging is essential.

> *<u>Writing</u> is the hardest way of <u>earning</u> a <u>living</u>, with the possible exception of <u>wrestling</u> alligators.*—Olin Miller

Infinitive. *To* + the present tense of a verb.

> *In a hierarchy every employee tends <u>to rise</u> to his level of incompetence.*—Laurence Peter

In a *split infinitive*, a word or phrase comes between *to* and the verb.

Split: They were asked to promptly complete the questionnaire.

Improved: They were asked to complete the questionnaire promptly.

Acceptable: We expect to more than double sales next year.

Inflection. Changes in the form of a word to show grammatical functions such as case, voice, person, mood, tense, and number. Thus, inflection of the pronoun *I* to *we* shows the change from singular to plural; inflection of *I* to *me* shows the change from nominative to objective case.

Interjection. A word or phrase that expresses strong feelings; an exclamation.

My word!   Holy mackerel!   How about that!   Wow!

Metaphor. The implicit comparison of concepts by substituting one concept for another in order to suggest their similarity. "The dawn of civilization" indirectly compares dawn to the early days of civilization. "The long arm of the law" gives law a human body in order to illustrate a similarity of function. (See p. 85.)

Writing, like life itself, is a voyage of discovery.—Henry Miller

Misplaced Modifier. Incorrect placement of a modifier which produces a misleading meaning. (See p. 122.)

Misplaced: Over one million Americans have a heart attack every year.
Correct: Every year over one million Americans have a heart attack.

Mood. The change made in a verb to show whether it makes a statement (*indicative mood*), is a command (*imperative mood*), or expresses a condition contrary to fact (*subjunctive mood*). (See p. 124.)

Noun. A word that names things. "Things" can be physical objects (table, pen), abstract concepts (humor, truth), actions (writing, scratching), substances (air, water), measures (centimeter, inch), places (street, factory), persons (reporter, mechanic), and so on.

Proper nouns refer to a specific person, place, or thing (Michelangelo, Houston, World War II) and are capitalized.

Parallel construction. Using grammatically parallel forms (e.g., infinitives or nouns) to emphasize the similarity or relatedness of ideas.
Unparallel: The power to tax involves the power of destruction.
Parallel: *The power to tax involves the power to destroy.*
—John Marshall

Participle. A verb form used as an adjective. (See Gerund.)

> an <u>inspiring</u> lecture   the <u>outraged</u> electorate
> a <u>worn</u> collar   a <u>frozen</u> dessert

> The <u>debugging</u> procedure took only a few minutes.

Parts of Speech. The classification of words according to the function they perform in a sentence: noun, pronoun, verb, adjective, adverb, preposition, conjunction, and interjection. The definition of each part of speech appears at its alphabetical entry.

Person. The speaker is the first person (*I, we*), the person spoken to is the second person (*you*), and the person or thing spoken of is the third person (*he, she, they, it*).

Phrase. A group of words that has no subject or predicate and that functions as if it were a single word.

> Turn right <u>at the signal</u>. (prepositional phrase)

> <u>Knowing the subject thoroughly</u>, she was quick to respond. (participial phrase)

Predicate. A group of words that makes a statement or asks a question about the subject of a sentence. A simple predicate consists of a verb; a complete predicate includes verbs, modifiers, objects, and complements.

> *A student <u>can win twelve letters at a university without learning how to write one</u>.* —Robert Maynard Hutchins

Prefix. A word element that is placed in front of a root word, thereby changing or modifying the meaning.

> <u>re</u>claim   <u>mis</u>print   <u>macro</u>cosm   <u>un</u>easy
> <u>dis</u>proportionate   <u>pre</u>dispose   <u>in</u>edible

Preposition. A word that shows the relationship between a noun and the object of the preposition. In the sentence "She put the check in the envelope," *in* is the preposition that shows the relationship between the noun *check* and the object of the preposition *envelope*.

> *The buck stops <u>with</u> the guy who signs the checks.*
> —Rupert Murdoch

Pronoun. A word that takes the place of a noun and is used in order to avoid cumbersome repetition. (See p. 118.) Pronouns are classified as follows:

Personal: *I, you, he, she, it* (sing.)
we, you, they (pl.)

and their inflected forms (e.g., *me, her, them, ours*).

> *The very fact that we make such a to-do over golden weddings indicates our amazement at human endurance. The celebration is more in the nature of a reward for stamina.* —Ilka Chase

Relative: *who, which, that,* and compounds like *whoever*. Relative pronouns relate one part of a sentence to a word in another part.

> *A government that robs Peter to pay Paul can always depend on the support of Paul.* —G. B. Shaw

Indefinite: *any, some, each, every,* and compounds with *-body* and *-one*, such as *no one, everyone, somebody,* and *nobody.*

> *Everyone has talent. What is rare is the courage to follow the talent to the dark place where it leads.* —Erica Jong

Reflexive and Intensive: *myself, themselves,* and others formed by adding *-self* or *-selves* to a personal pronoun.

> *Tact is the ability to describe others as they see themselves.*
> —Abraham Lincoln

Demonstrative: *this, that, these, those*

> That is the wrong answer.

Interrogative: *who, which, what*

> *Who shall guard the guardians themselves?* —Juvenal

Sentence. A combination of words that contains at least one subject and predicate (grammatical definition); a group of words that expresses a complete thought (popular definition).

Sentence structures are classified as follows.

Simple: One independent clause consisting of a subject and predicate; the sentence may have modifying phrases but no dependent clauses.

There is no abstract art. You must always start with something.
—Pablo Picasso

Compound: Two or more independent clauses.

Blessed are the young, for they shall inherit the national debt.
—Herbert Hoover

Complex: One independent and one or more dependent clauses.

When ideas fail, words come in very handy.—Johann Goethe

Power and violence are opposites; where one rules absolutely, the other is absent.—Hannah Arendt

Sentence functions are categorized as follows.

Declarative: Makes an assertion

Interrogative: Asks a question

Imperative: Issues a command

Exclamatory: Expresses a strong feeling

Success is simply a matter of luck.   Ask any failure.—Earl Wilson

(declarative)   (imperative)

(interrogative)

How can they tell?—Dorothy Parker, on hearing of Calvin Coolidge's death

Don't trust anyone over thirty!—Mario Savio

(exclamatory)

Sentence faults result from trying to crowd too much into a sentence (*comma splice, fused sentence*) or from failing to have enough in a sentence (*fragment*).

Comma Splice: Two independent clauses joined only by a comma.

Wrong: We are temporarily out of widgets, however we expect a shipment within two weeks.

Right: We are temporarily out of widgets; however, we expect a shipment within two weeks.   *or*

Right: We are temporarily out of widgets. However, we expect a shipment within two weeks.

Fused Sentence: Two independent clauses with no punctuation connecting them.

Wrong: We expect immediate payment otherwise we will turn your account over to a collection agency.

Right: We expect immediate payment; otherwise we will turn your account over to a collection agency.

Fragment: A partial sentence that either lacks a verb or fails to express a complete thought.

Wrong: Whenever I think I know all the answers.

Right: Whenever I think I know all the answers, life asks a few more questions.

Fragments are acceptable in questions and answers, for occasional emphasis ("Not likely."), in transitions ("On to the next point."), and in definitions.

> *The two oldest professions in the world—ruined by amateurs.*
> —Alexander Woollcott

Simile. A direct comparison using the word *like* or *as*. (See p. 74.)

> *A woman without a man is like a fish without a bicycle.*
> —Gloria Steinem

Suffix. A word element added to the end of a root word.

genocide   boredom   fortify   backward

Synonym. A word similar in meaning to another word. (See Antonym.)

invisible/unseen   handbook/manual   hazard/danger

Tense. The form of a verb that shows distinctions in time: present, past, future, present perfect, past perfect, future perfect. (See p. 123.)

Verb. A word that asserts that something exists, has certain characteristics, or acts in a certain way. Verbs change form to indicate time (she will speak, he spoke), person (I speak, he speaks), or mood (Speak!). (See p. 123 ff.)

Linking verbs, such as *to be, to appear, to become*, and *to seem* serve as connections between the subject and its *complement*. (See Complement.)

> *Pollution is nothing but resources we're not harvesting.*
> —R. Buckminster Fuller

Transitive verbs require a direct object to complete their meaning.

> *Big girls need big diamonds.*—Margaux Hemingway

Intransitive verbs do not require an object.

> *Society attacks early when the individual is helpless.*
> —B.F. Skinner

Voice. The form of the verb used to express the relation between the subject and the action expressed by the verb.

In the *active voice*, the subject performs the action of the verb.

> *Fiction reveals truths that reality obscures.*—Jessamyn West

In the *passive voice*, the subject is the object of the action of the verb.

> *Flesh was the reason why oil painting was invented.*
> —Willem deKooning (See p. 79.)

Bibliography

The Chicago Manual of Style, 13th ed., Chicago: Univ. of Chicago Press, 1982.

Cook, Claire Kehrwald, *Line by Line: How to Improve Your Own Writing,* Boston: Houghton Mifflin Co., 1985.

Jacobi, Ernst, *Writing at Work*, Berkeley, CA: Ten Speed Press, 1985.

Keenan, John, *Feel Free to Write*, New York: John Wiley & Sons, 1982.

Roman, Kenneth and Joel Raphaelson, *Writing That Works*, New York: Harper & Row, 1981.

Sorrels, Bobbye D., *The Nonsexist Communicator*, Englewood Cliffs, NJ: Prentice-Hall, Inc., 1983.

Strunk, William Jr. and E. B. White, *The Elements of Style*, 3rd ed., New York: The Macmillan Co., 1979.

Success with Words: A Guide to the American Language, Pleasantville, NY: The Reader's Digest Association, 1983.

Venolia, Jan, *Better Letters: A Handbook of Business and Personal Correspondence*, Berkeley, CA: Ten Speed Press, 1982.

Venolia, Jan, *Write Right! A Desk Drawer Digest of Punctuation, Grammar & Style,* Berkeley, CA: Ten Speed Press, 1982.

Words into Type, 3rd ed., Englewood Cliffs, NJ: Prentice-Hall, Inc., 1983.

Index